Carly-Jay Metcalfe is a Queensland-based writer. Her work has been published in *Kill Your Darlings*, *The Guardian* and *TEXT Journal*. She is a passionate advocate for organ donation and for more honest conversations around dying and death.

First published 2024 by University of Queensland Press
PO Box 6042, St Lucia, Queensland 4067 Australia

University of Queensland Press (UQP) acknowledges the Traditional Owners and their custodianship of the lands on which UQP operates. We pay our respects to their Ancestors and their descendants, who continue cultural and spiritual connections to Country. We recognise their valuable contributions to Australian and global society.

uqp.com.au
reception@uqp.com.au

Cover design by Christa Moffitt
Cover photograph by Shutterstock
Author photograph by Sharon Danzig
Typeset in 13/16 by Perpetua MT Std by Post Pre-press Group, Brisbane
Printed in Australia by McPherson's Printing Group

Quotes from Stephen Jenkinson in the 2008 documentary *Griefwalker* reprinted with the permission of Tim Wilson and the National Film Board of Canada.

University of Queensland Press is supported by the Queensland Government through Arts Queensland.

University of Queensland Press is assisted by the Australian Government through Creative Australia, its principal arts investment and advisory body.

A catalogue record for this book is available from the National Library of Australia.

ISBN 978 0 7022 6835 9 (pbk)
ISBN 978 0 7022 6944 8 (epdf)
ISBN 978 0 7022 6945 5 (epub)

University of Queensland Press uses papers that are natural, renewable and recyclable products made from wood grown in well-managed forests and other controlled sources. The logging and manufacturing processes conform to the environmental regulations of the country of origin.

Breath

Carly-Jay Metcalfe

UQP

For my parents and my sister,
for always carrying me so tenderly.

'Death smiles at us all; all we can do is smile back.'

— Marcus Aurelius

I AM DYING. I KNOW that I'm dying, despite not having been told by my doctors that I am dying. I know I am dying because I'm in the dying room. It's quiet, and people slip in and out as if they were never here. For what seems like the longest time, I've been a body in a bed – a bundle of atrophied muscle and chalky bones, the timbre of my breath thick and craggy. I feel the yawn marching in my winter lungs and hear the final infection coming, slow at first, then roaring like a diesel engine into my living corpse, filling it with blood and pus and mucus. I can taste my death in the internal suppurations I cough up, the smell like rotting oysters.

In hospital, everything hums – the burr of machines as they pump IV antibiotics through infirm bodies, the buzz of fluorescent lights, the thrum of a helicopter landing on the helipad. Far from an idyllic symphony, the fizz and crackle of people moving, the whispers of lost conversations and last breaths is disconcerting.

And now, those last breaths I hear are my own.

Old men hobble into my room with bottles full of steaming piss, their saggy, hairless balls poking out of their hospital gowns. There's little room for elegance in decay. It's an odd thing, being able to taste your own death. For years, X-rays have shown the infection blooming like a stain across my chest, but I've never tasted it or felt the pain so acutely. If you've ever had a baby elephant trample your rib cage as you struggle to breathe underwater through an occluded straw – this is what it feels like to die. There's no talk of palliative care because people like me aren't palliated: we don't have time – death comes upon us suddenly.

I decide it's easier to die, simply because it's impossible to go on. It will be painful, yes, but easy. I don't have questions because I've seen this situation play out many times before; I have always known this is how I would end. But there's one thing I want to do before I dip into the inevitable coma, and that's to see my friends one last time. To say goodbye, but mostly to say: I love you; thank you for loving me.

I am ready to die. I'm ready to let go of the world, but the world wants me to stay. So, I do. Like an unarticulated vow, I stay.

Later, Dad will tell me that when he and Mum get home from the hospital that night, he can't settle. He senses that they're going to be summoned back to the ward, but he can't work out if it's to say goodbye or because I'll finally get 'the call'. So, instead, he paces cypress floorboards, tries to watch TV, smokes dozens of cigarettes, drinks endless cups of instant coffee.

It's just before midnight, and I'm sleeping upright in my hospital bed. I can't lay flat because my lungs are swimming in infection; I get a sense of how it must feel to drown, and drown slowly.

The shrillness of the phone slices through the smell of decay that's been hanging like an invisible curtain in my room for weeks. I presume it's my boyfriend, Ollie, calling to see if he can come up and sleep in my bed, although he usually just materialises in my doorway, drunk and happy.

But it's not Ollie. It's my cystic fibrosis (CF) doctor, Simon, and because I'm levitating on a billowing plume of morphine, I think how lovely it is that, despite the hour, he's calling for a leisurely chat.

'Hey Simon, how are you?'

I can sense him smiling through the phone. 'I've got great news, mate. We've got a set of lungs for you.'

'Oh my god. Really?'

'Really.'

'Holy fuck.'

'Ha! That's exactly what your sister said.'

My thoughts move to my sister, Nikki, as I imagine her at home, tripping over in the darkness as she reaches for the phone, her blood pumping with such force and vim that she glows.

My mind whirrs as Simon explains that I'm going to be transferred by ambulance from the Mater Hospital to the Prince Charles. When I hang up, a couple of the nurses gather in my doorway, tears spilling down their cheeks. My night nurse, Daisy, who has seen me fade from a firecracker of a girl, helps me pour my child-sized body into a pair of jeans and wrangle on my blue Chuck Taylors.

I call Ollie. We're in the age before everyone owns a mobile phone, and I'm glad he answers – he's not long home from a night out with the boys. He sobers up in record time.

'Oh my god,' he says slowly. 'I'll be there, babe. At the hospital. And for you. Holy shit. I love you.'

Next, I call my best friend, Laura.

'Holy fuck! This is amazing! I'm leaving right now! FUCK!'

I leave her in charge of calling our group of friends before she bolts out of her house and runs a red light on the way to the hospital. Dad runs two.

I'm wheeled downstairs to the emergency department; outside, the ambulance sits in its bay like a hearse waiting to transport the living dead. During the night, squalls of rain have moved down into the city from the ranges. As we drive over glistening ribbons of road, a solar eclipse stretches its way across the Earth. A jolt of flavour lands unexpectedly on my tongue. Initially, I think it's humidity, but I know rain doesn't taste metallic – it's blood in my mouth from coughing, and I wonder if it's the last thing I'll ever taste.

When I arrive at The Prince Charles Hospital, Mum, Dad and Nikki are waiting for me, as is Ollie. In an act of drunken devotion, he has bought flowers and a box of chocolates from a service station, even though I have to fast before surgery. We're taken up to the ward, and more friends arrive: my besties Bec, Tammy, Laura, Sharon and Mel, who've been my anchors since we started primary school. Then Dylan, Lana, Shae (and later, her boyfriend, Dave) squeeze in with Ollie's mum, Claire, his brother, Matthew, and his mates Toby and Paul. My sister's best friend, Samantha, arrives, and finally Alicia, the photographer who will be documenting my surgery.

A living, breathing Nurse Ratched storms into the room and admonishes us for being noisy, her voice curdling with anger. 'Patients are trying to sleep!'

'She's only having a fucking transplant,' says Lana.

I smile at Lana as the nurse leaves.

'I couldn't give a *fuck* about the other patients,' Lana says, and we all laugh.

It's impossible to stay quiet when something of this magnitude is happening, and so Nurse Ratched returns again and again over the next few hours.

During the night, my transplant physician, Scott, joins us, holding handfuls of paperwork. He looks flustered but excited. Only twelve hours earlier, he was apologising.

'I'm sorry,' he'd said over the phone.

'It's okay,' I'd replied.

'I'm sorry we haven't been able to get you lungs. I'm sorry we haven't been able to save you.'

'It's okay,' I'd repeated.

While his words should have been shocking, I found them strangely comforting; perhaps it was the unexpected apology from a doctor that took me off-guard. Now, news of the transplant feels like an unbelievable about-face, somewhat espionage-like.

'It's not going to be easy,' he tells me.

'I know.'

'But it'll be worth it.'

'I hope so.'

'It will be. It's just not going to be easy.'

Over the course of that evening, I say goodbye to my friends. My high-school friend Alex, now living in Melbourne, has her mum bring me a prayer of St Benedictine, but the most visceral memory is how hard Tammy hugs me. It hurts, and I can't breathe, but I can't breathe anyway and at least it makes me feel alive. I don't want to let go.

As the night ticks on, I'm moved to a two-bed room and my friends disperse into a waiting room. The only people allowed in the room are my parents, my sister, Ollie and Alicia. A lovely nurse called Sonia hands me a towel, a surgical sponge, a gown, a pair of paper undies, a paper hat and a razor, so I can shower and prep for surgery.

'I won't need the razor,' I say.

'Oh, but … oh, okay!' We both laugh.

After my shower, Ollie helps me put on my paper undies.

'This is strange,' he says in his Ollie drawl. 'I've never had to put these *on*.'

Mum and Nikki overhear and laugh, and for the first time I am thankful that Dad is – quite literally – half deaf.

Suddenly, I feel like I'm about to throw up, so Sonia gives me a metal bowl that I proceed to wear as a hat.

At 7.30 am I'm taken downstairs to the operating suites. I've been nothing but calm the entire morning and remain so as I hug my parents and sister goodbye and give Ollie a final kiss. As I'm wheeled into the operating theatre I'm sitting up on the gurney, but when I glance back, I see everyone there and I begin to howl. I'm howling because I'm certain I am going to die on that table, and I'll never see my loved ones again.

This is my clarion call.

MY MUM HAD CONCERNS ABOUT me not long after my birth.

She's salty.

She won't feed.

She won't gain weight.

She poos all the time and it stinks. It's not like normal baby poo.

Her stomach is so big.

She can't hear. We think she's deaf.

My parents would walk around me like a marching band, clanging pots and pans to gauge my reaction. For the first nine weeks of my life, Mum and Dad were confounded because I was not at all like their first baby – wriggly as a worm, screaming for the breast and getting chubbier with each feed. I was a happy baby, but a whippet of a thing and had failure to thrive. I was born with a chest infection and even the matron commented on how dreadful my cough was. Mum's maternal instinct was telling her that something was wrong. Her family weren't exactly sympathetic.

Jewel, you're being paranoid.

You need to settle down – every baby is different.

Stop worrying.

She'll be fine.

When my parents brought me home from hospital, Mum said

that I rattled; I would shake so violently when I coughed that my body would move all the way down the bassinet I was laying in.

'I felt like there was something different when I was pregnant with you, but I didn't know what – it was just ... different.' As I would later learn, I was overdue by a fortnight and Mum was so terrified about having her waters broken and being induced that, with her legs in stirrups, her waters didn't just break – they exploded and hit a wall three metres away. The nurses had never seen anything like it. It's family lore that Mum held Dad in a headlock for three hours, screaming, 'You'll never do this to me again!' I was born at 11.43 pm on New Year's Eve.

⚘

Life is made. And then it is unmade.

One should never doubt a mother's instinct, but that wasn't going to get my parents a diagnosis. Cystic fibrosis (CF) – a disease that affects the lungs, liver, pancreas and digestive system – was the first thing I was tested for. A sweat test was done, which in 1977 wasn't as scientific as it is today. Back then, to do the sweat test Mum had to wrap me in blankets and hold me in the back seat of our car in the searing February heat. When I asked Mum if I cried, she said I just gaggled away happily.

After the sweat test, the doctor said to my parents, somewhat surreptitiously, 'I think she has a fibrocystic condition.'

One day in March, Mum took a call from our neighbours' house (my parents didn't yet have a telephone). The doctor called a meeting at his rooms in north Brisbane, where it was confirmed I had CF. Instead of feeling vindicated and free from the judgements of her family, my mother felt like someone had thrown a burning axe through her heart.

In the 1980s, children with CF had a high morbidity rate,

rarely living into adolescence. My parents were told that I wouldn't survive infancy. It wasn't a life-limiting illness so much as a life-ending one. My parents left the doctor's office with a crushing feeling of dread. They may have had a diagnosis, but their baby daughter had a death sentence. They cried all the way home.

While humans have certainly died from CF for thousands of years, the first clear references to the disease extend back only a few centuries. European folklore from the Middle Ages warned, 'Woe is the child who tastes salty from a kiss on the brow, for he is cursed, and soon must die.' In medical texts as early as 1595, references have been found linking salty skin and damage to the pancreas with death in infants who were 'hexed' or 'bewitched'. Scholars have long speculated that Polish composer Frederic Chopin (1810–1849) had CF. Chopin died of respiratory failure after a lifetime of malabsorption and lung infections, but given he survived into his thirties – which was unheard of for a person with CF in the nineteenth century – he may have just been a carrier of the gene.

Since it is the deadliest genetic disease in the Western world, a simple explanation of CF is warranted. For a person to be born with CF, both parents must be carriers of the defective CF gene. It's known that one in twenty-five people are carriers of the gene, and if both parents are carriers there's a one in four chance their child will be born with CF. It's a disease that, up until recently, mainly affected Caucasians, but as bloodlines have combined, CF now also exists in places like Japan, India and Africa.

Often, CF babies are born with bowel obstructions necessitating urgent surgery, while others – like me – aren't born with any acute gastrointestinal issues apart from malabsorption. Babies are tested for CF at birth with a heel prick. If the results contain increased levels of a substance called immunoreactive trypsinogen (IRT), which is secreted in the pancreas, a sweat test is done to check the level of sodium in their skin.

When I was born – or even when I was growing up, for that matter – CF wasn't an adult disease. This is because it killed children and teenagers before they could reach adulthood. In the 1980s, there were only ever one or two adults on the CF ward in the adults' hospital because most of them never made it out of the children's hospital.

Rumours of cures for CF – particularly media beat-ups – have always felt cruel. There is nothing as devastating as false hope. The first time I heard there 'would be a cure within a few years', I would have been seven. I telephoned my best friend, Karen, told her the news, and danced around my parents' living room to A-ha's 'Take on Me'. And I remember thinking, 'My friends won't die, and I'll be able to dance without getting breathless and I won't have to have any more needles.' When a research team, led by Doctor Lap-See Tsui finally isolated the defective gene in 1989, this was real and tangible on a monumental scale. It was a technology we could *use*, and there was hope there would be a cure within five to ten years. But in the meantime, friends still died agonising deaths, and there was a surge in babies born with CF.

When I think about my childhood, I feel a rush of happiness. My parents did their best to normalise our lives. I wasn't treated as special, even if I did have a limited life span. We went to the beach, often for Christmas and Easter, where I would spend summer days pretending to be a mermaid. My favourite feeling in the world was floating in the sea – rising on the crest of a wave just before it broke and revelling in the violent tug back down to the sand. I have always felt a magnetic pull towards water. Striding out of the ocean, I never tired of feeling my skin crusting and tightening with salt as it dried under the sun.

Yet even at an early age I was dealing with adult concepts. And as hard as my parents tried to keep me tethered to childhood, I would find myself drifting. I had all the normality Mum and Dad could give me – school, homework, dinner at the table every night, chores and a set of manners to rival royalty. But every time I got a chest infection, I would go into hospital for what was called a 'tune up'.

With every hospital admission, as I climbed onto my bed with its stiffly laundered white sheets, I wondered if I was filling the space of a child who had just died; in all likelihood a child who I knew. More than once, I'd felt the breath of my friends' departures, the timbre of their spirit winding down, the sad predictability of history repeating.

Growing up with CF was akin to living a double life. I lived my normal life at home, had my normal friends at normal school, and did normal things. Then, when I went into hospital for weeks at a time, I had my hospital life, replete with hospital school and hospital friends. The hospital school was where I liked to be. Whenever I went in for a tune up, my incredible hospital schoolteacher, Suzanne, would call my school and they would fax through reams of schoolwork for me to do. Study was my escape and my bed was often covered in books. When a friend died, either in the next bed or next room, I would go to normal school the next day as though nothing had happened.

Four words encapsulated my childhood hospital admissions: 'You have terrible veins.' It was something I always heard from doctors and phlebotomists. I never had veins that were adequate for blood collection or intravenous access for IV antibiotics. My veins were small and difficult to locate, they would roll, disappear, blow and tissue. One of my earliest memories was of razor blades being stabbed into the tips of my five-year-old fingers to collect blood because after at least six attempts with a needle the phlebotomist simply couldn't find another vein to bleed.

Doctors would try to cannulate my feet, and the pain always felt more than the 'sharp scratch' they described as they bored the needle through my young skin. It was a searing intrusion. As a little girl, my favourite blood lady was Joyce. Joyce had a glorious bouffant that defied gravity. She was gentle, kind and usually managed to find a vein – and blood – on the first puncture. I learnt to ask for Joyce when I was only six; otherwise, I knew I was in for a world of pain.

There is a day in my memory that plays like a movie on a loop. I am in the treatment room at the Royal Children's Hospital. It is a room of cold steel with a long, thin bed that folds down off the wall. I hop off the bed after deciding that six failed cannulation attempts is enough. I am in pain and the doctor keeps grabbing my hands and pulling my arms, trying to slap a tourniquet on. If you can conjure up a skinnier, taller, inferior version of Gene Wilder with a thin moustache and a bulging Adam's apple, you'll have a fair idea of what the doctor looked like.

The nurses allow me to phone my mum, who hasn't yet come in for her daily visit. As always, Mum drops everything to drive to the hospital. When Mum arrives, we stand in the hallway of Turner Ward, the doctor tearing strips off me.

'You need to start taking responsibility for your illness!' he bellows down the hall, his spittle speckling my eight-year-old face.

Mum, ever gracious, takes me by the hand and walks me out to the park where we sit on the swings alongside the old bus permanently parked there, rusted-out and teeming with tetanus. She pulls me onto her lap and we both cry.

After this incident, Mum made a complaint to the head of the hospital. She remembers speaking to a kind man in a dark suit who apologised with a sincerity my mother had not experienced from a doctor before. The offending doctor, like many of his colleagues in the era before medicine became about health care, had elevated himself to messianic status. When 'Gene Wilder' eventually delivered an apology, rippling with insincerity, he asked if there was anything he could do to make it up to me.

'Let me cannulate you,' I said.

My friend David Kelly, who was in the same ward and also had CF, thought this was a grand idea. David would have been about twelve at the time, so he was a bit older than me.

'And I get to have a go after Carly,' he said, his glee evident in his velvety South African accent.

The doctor lay his lithe body on the treatment room bed. I took a tourniquet and selected the thickest-gauged needle on the trolley. The dark brown soles of his leather shoes moved around on the bed awkwardly, his feet in little death throes.

David's eyes lit up. 'Buckle up, bitch.'

I tightened the tourniquet, found a plump vein, swabbed the doctor's skin with an alcohol wipe and drove the needle in with precision. I got it first go. The doctor cried. I removed the tourniquet, pulled out the needle, leaving the plastic cannula in place, attached a tube and a bung, and taped it down like a professional. After all, 'Gene Wilder' deserved the full treatment.

'It's not that hard,' I said. Not in a nasty way, but in a factual way.

'Maybe you're just not a very good doctor,' David tells him from the bottom of the bed.

But it wasn't all suffering. When he was in a rush one night, Dad brought me up some Kentucky Fried Chicken. I sat at the table guiltily eating my chicken while the other kids poked the stodge around on their plates. The next time he visited, he brought up enough for the other five kids, and he became a kind of hero.

Mum and Dad tell me that I never complained. Every needle, every painful treatment, every admission to hospital – it was as if I was happy to accept my fate. When I knew I was going home after a couple of weeks in hospital, I'd have my bags packed at 7.00 am, knowing that Mum and I would have to wait for hours to get the all-clear before we were discharged, and then spend another hour in pharmacy waiting for my medication. Like any kid leaving hospital after more than a fortnight, I was euphoric. Even as a toddler, in the car on the drive home, Mum would always say, 'Nearly home', and I'd echo from the back seat, 'Leeely home!'

I AM TWENTY-ONE WHEN I have my double lung transplant. In 1998 it was still the subject of dreams and legends. I needed one to live and I was fairly sure I would die on the waiting list; the technology was all very new. In a macabre way, my family looked hopefully to public holidays because that's when the prospect of car crashes, and available lungs, would increase. When Ollie and I went away at Easter – notorious for fatalities – I strapped my beeper to my cut-offs. We would later learn that lungs are often squashed on impact, rendering them unviable for transplant. Realising this, I feel equal parts guilt and disgust, and it makes me hyper-conscious of one brutal fact: I'm waiting for someone else to die so I may live.

One night, as I cough up half a cup of blood, my father vows to find a triathlete with perfect lung function to assassinate.

'You'd need to know their tissue type,' I say through bloodied lips, as if it is a reasonable plan.

'I'll take my chances,' he says, sucking on a cigarette.

It is ghoulish, but gallows humour is how I get through. If you don't laugh, you die. Lifelong illness bludgeons your sense of identity and safety. In her book *The Year of Magical Thinking*, Joan Didion's belief that no-one and nothing will keep her or her daughter Quintana safe is something I feel deep in my bones. I am not safe. I have never been safe. I will never be safe.

In a myth of my own making, I've always believed that my broad swimmer's shoulders mean I have large lungs. The scans I have in my pre-transplant work-up show that, in fact, my lungs are small. At our first meeting, my transplant physician, Scott, explains that I might need a child's lungs and I could be in for a long wait. This thought sickens me to the point where I consider taking myself off the transplant list. I don't know it then, but I will eventually discover that my donor was a grown woman.

Myth has been a consistent thread running through my life. There is a story arc in myths known as 'the hero's journey' or the 'monomyth' that fits my narrative neatly. In its most popular incarnation it's an arc that writer Joseph Campbell appropriated from James Joyce's *Finnegans Wake*. It begins with a departure, followed by initiation, and ends with the triumphant return of the hero who has grown into a superior human being. There are over a dozen substages in between, but in a nutshell the hero is called to adventure only for it to become a trauma. Ultimately, the hero returns with a renewed spiritual purpose, ready to pass their wisdom on to the community.

In his memoir about heart disease and cancer, *The Wounded Storyteller*, sociologist Arthur Frank divides illness narratives into three types: restitution, in which the person returns to their previous state of health; chaos, in which all life events are contingent and where there is no control; and quest, in which illness is seen as some kind of spiritual journey. The idea of restitution implies that when a healthy body becomes ill, it will at some stage, inevitably, return to health. In most cases of illness, there is remission or a cure where a person fully recovers from what has ailed them. But what about when things don't get better?

Doctor Peter Levine writes about 'meeting and embracing trauma' in his book *Trauma and Memory*. I've certainly met my trauma, but it's not something I've ever embraced. How do you embrace something that hurts you? I've never seen myself as a victim, but just by existing, trauma has punched itself into my every cell. The fact is, I couldn't embrace my trauma. It didn't only hurt me, it hurt my parents, my sister, my friends with CF. Plus, there was a lot of time to process the enormity of what was going on. I do have a catalogue of traumatic memories, and for me, it's easier to remember than it is to forget. As Aristotle committed to papyrus a couple of thousand years ago, 'memory is the scribe of the soul'.

⚘

When I am intubated and my sedation is lowered to wake me up, I point out my first words on an alphabet board.

'Am I alive?'

Everyone giggles and says yes.

Then I spell out, 'I love you' before I am sedated again.

Turner Ward was a ward of five cubicles – A to E. A trinity of linoleum, stainless steel and suffering, it was a waiting room for death within the Royal Children's Hospital. 'A' cube was where the kids with cancer went. 'E' cube was where the kids with CF went. In the 1980s, kids with cancer were rare specimens in the true sense of the phrase: there weren't many of them, and they were treated as medical anomalies. Black sheets of plastic covered the windows of their room. As kids looking in from the park outside, we deduced it could mean only one of three things – that the cancer kids couldn't bear sunlight, that the drugs they were on made them light-sensitive, or that they didn't want people looking in. As I learnt later, it was all three.

Cancer in the early 1980s was stigmatised – much like AIDS – and kids were assigned a death sentence with their diagnosis. The book cupboard – filled with infantile Golden Books and old, ratty romance novels – was lodged near the nurses' station between A and B cubes. The motivation behind a visit to the book cupboard was to get as close to the cancer kids as we could, but when we snuck up the hallway on the pretext of wanting a book, we were swatted away like flies.

What were we hoping to see with this morbid fusion of curiosity and scalding guilt? Kids with bald, satiny heads and barrelled chests, tentacles of tubes spilling from their tiny bodies? Nurses would emerge from the room in full universal precautions – long-sleeved gowns, masks, goggles and gloves – which felt mildly dystopian. We surmised that this was to prevent the cancer kids from getting even sicker, yet the idea of nurses spreading germs to us didn't garner much concern.

Nor did some of our other pastimes. I recall playing with mercury from deliberately broken thermometers, the silver baubles rolling across the floor with barely the touch of my skin as they broke off into smaller particles before disappearing into the floor. This became as literal as it was metaphorical, this slipping away. Everyone and everything turned to mercury: there one moment and gone the next. One day I was touching them, the next they had vanished, and I would find myself front and centre at their funeral.

Attached by a short walkway to Turner Ward was Patterson Ward, an isolation ward for infectious diseases, where I was dumped if my lungs were colonising a different strain of bug from the run-of-the-mill *Pseudomonas aeruginosa*. When I was eleven, I got shingles, which sent me into paroxysms of itching. Weeping sores bloomed across my forehead and into my left eye, and doctors worried that I would lose my sight. I remember torches being shone into my eye as my head was held deadlocked by men in white coats, like a cow in a cattle crush.

Nights in the Adelaide Billing Ward at the Royal Children's Hospital, my next home away from home, were a flurry of activity. With more sick kids than the nurses knew what to do with, we'd sneak out and walk to the adults' hospital to buy sweets at the canteen, after which we would break into the new wing of the hospital, which had been built for orthopaedic and burns patients. From there, it was basically a free-for-all, where we got to do all the things we were forbidden to do – like jumping up onto the desks, dancing on ledges or racing armchairs around the empty clinic rooms. CF kids were notorious hellraisers, and we'd desecrate every space we could get ourselves into. If our CF compatriot Cameron Smith was in for an admission, he would have his video camera with him, and we'd make videos to songs like 'Bad Medicine' by Bon Jovi. We created all the choreography, and somehow Cameron managed to skilfully edit the film in hospital. A few years after the videos were shot, I was the only one still alive. Years later, the videotapes disappeared and fell into CF folklore – our history erased like we were never there.

Adelaide Billing – the ward and the woman herself – made fine fodder for hospital folklore. I was never in any doubt that Matron Billing still marched up and down the halls of the ward of an evening. Stories were passed down to us about strange goings-on, as well as photos with her ghostly likeness in the background, her hand on the shoulders of other nurses. In spectral form, she would check the temperatures of newborns, rearrange toys in their cots, and settle crotchety babies.

Reading was my cherished pastime; an exquisite pull that took me away from what was happening in my day-to-day life. Books were better than medicine, better than physio and IV antibiotics.

My friend Ineka recommended two books that had an impact on me as a kid – Colin Thiele's *The Undercover Secret* and Louise Fitzhugh's classic *Harriet the Spy*. So much so that I created my own detective agency with a friend, where we set about solving cases the police weren't getting anywhere with. I even found myself a reporter-style notebook and a magnifying glass. I wore a long olive-green vinyl coat with a Fedora tipped to one side. With my uniform and notebook, I would skulk around the neighbourhood, and the hospital, writing everything down. And yes, *everything* was suspicious.

I have fond memories of Ineka reading after the lights had been switched off, which was the only time that afforded us a chance to settle or decompress after a day of missed cannulations, being held down on the long plank of a table in the treatment room, or after a run-in with the matron, 'Feral Meryl'. Long after being told to scramble into our beds, Ineka would bide her time until the cubicle was still, waiting to hear the gaggle of nurses move to the other end of the ward to gossip and write in charts at the front desk.

You wouldn't see Ineka because there was nothing of her, but you could always hear the unmistakable rattle in her throat and chest. She would read by the window, the only light thrown down by the moon or the lights in the park outside. Everyone else was asleep, but I would watch her read. I wouldn't have been older than six when we first met, yet I still remember her silhouette – a little girl with a curved back cradling the spine of a book, her hands shaking from Ventolin, the angular shape of her face, her delicate wrists and her thick dark-blonde bob. Ineka knew she didn't have long on this Earth, as did the nurses, so why couldn't they just let her read? It was something I could never understand.

I was eleven when Ineka died; she was only fifteen. Her death was the loss of my last shred of innocence.

Mum drove me to the hospital to say goodbye. We chatted with Ineka's mum, Trish, in the kitchenette and then I walked up the hall to the dying room, opened the door, and closed it gently behind me. I pulled a chair over to the side of Ineka's bed and sat down. I took her hand and interlaced our fingers.

'Ineka, it's me.'

She was lying on her side in the foetal position, lips cracked, an oversized oxygen mask strapped to her face. Her eyes fluttered as she whispered my name.

'Shh, don't speak. I love you.'

Her last whispered words to me were, 'I love you,' and she managed to summon the strength to squeeze my hand one last time. I stroked her hair, brushed the back of my palm across her cheek, kissed her on the forehead and hand, and said goodbye. After leaving the dying room, my skin was coated with the stench and the bone-crunching pain of hearing Ineka's almost final breaths.

Returning to the kitchenette, my mum and Trish were talking and crying. Trish reached into a bag and pulled out the purple wool cardigan she'd knitted for Ineka.

'Ine wanted you to have this,' she said, handing me the cardigan she had knitted with such love and care. The three of us huddled together and cried.

I still have that cardigan. It still fits me. I still wear it.

⚘

When Haley Joel Osment's character in *The Sixth Sense* whispered, 'I see dead people,' I felt a niggle of recognition because I see dead people, too. Not ghosts or spirits; I see my friends in spectral form even though many of them have been dead for over thirty-five years. Their presence has not faded with the passage of time. Instead, today – right here and now – some of them are more alive to me in death. Memories cut through like a bitter squall biting into the spine of a mountain; it is harder to forget than it is to remember. My friends occupy a space around me, offering a buffer of sorts – a soft place to land. Some days it feels like I am nursing the dead, ferrying them around with every thought and intention. Sometimes they invite themselves, shadowing me. Chunks of my childhood have been perforated out of my history like a primal yawn. Death has always been a corporeal experience for me; I feel emptier after each loss.

My dreams are all consuming, the people in them real. When I wake, they stay with me, tinging my day with their rituals, their clothes, their smell, their jokes, their cough, the way they brushed their hair, how they pirouetted on their heel as they left a room, their favourite songs. I never know if the dreams are a channel between them and me, or if they're just memories resurfacing with the veil of night. I try to sleep, surrounded by my friends.

My grief is only part of the story because it's a collective grief shared by my friends' parents, their siblings, partners and friends, and the doctors, nurses and physios who tried to save their lives. As a child and adolescent, most of my friends' deaths were identical. Some kids held on for weeks, while others only took a few days, but the end result was always the same: we were left breathing out our guilt in their absence.

I'm often asked, 'How did you get through it?'

'It can always be worse,' I say, because I have learnt that it almost always can be.

Those of us who left behind talked it out. We danced it out. We played loud music and head banged. We screamed it out in the park and into our pillows. We beat tennis balls with poorly strung plastic racquets and jumped on our beds. Other times, we were so overwrought by a binding sense of fear and guilt that no-one could speak at all. At night, when we were left with nothing but the darkness and were too frightened to close our eyes, whispers and awkward giggles echoed across the hospital room as we crawled into each other's beds. Eventually someone would pipe up and say, 'Who do you reckon's next?'

Because we never thought that it could be us. At least, that's what I told myself. My oxygen saturations were good, and I hadn't coughed up cupfuls of blood – yet. I was a good weight and wasn't on supplemental feeding – yet.

⚘

When I was fourteen, I started meditating after asking for a copy of Paul Wilson's *The Calm Technique* for Christmas. I liked to go down to our jetty, which floated on the river's surface, but it was the full moon that made me feel truly alive. When I sat cross-legged on the jetty, the high tide made it feel like I was levitating on water. It was my favourite place to be. In fact, anywhere along the river instantly lent me a feeling of peace I couldn't find anywhere else. I'd always been a water baby, learning to swim when Mum and Dad threw my sister and me in the pool to 'drown proof' us. Growing up, I was a very strong swimmer, but the older I got, the more my lungs let me down and the slower I went.

I went on to meditate all through high school, and I returned to it in my twenties. I can now get into a meditative state when I'm having medical procedures done; I take myself back to where I'm levitating on the water. I'm not sure if this ability has come through practise, necessity, or both. I rejoice in remembering the ordinary – the tin roof of our house flexing under the sun, mashed jacaranda flowers, half-eaten mangoes dropped by possums on their nocturnal travels.

If I wasn't at school or with my friends, I would often go for a walk along the river to my local park. I'd hop on a swing while I listened to mixtapes on my Walkman, which I'd shove indelicately down my pants, and throw my head back, my hair trailing in long ribbons on the wake of a river breeze. Summer meant lying in the sun with lemon juice in my hair, water-skiing and being thrown around on the surface of the water on an inner tube. Of course, there was physio, nebulisers, courses of antibiotics, antifungals, steroids and hospital admissions. I always seemed to be straddling two different worlds.

⚘

Over the years, there were a stream of regular fundraisers for the Queensland chapter of the Cystic Fibrosis Association (CFA). There was also the occasional special event put on for us, and in 1988 I found myself at an air show at the Amberley RAAF base. I was – by my standards – enormous. I had recently finished a course of high-dose steroids to settle my asthma, and when I look at photos from that day, what stands out the most (apart from my moon face and poorly self-administered haircut) is the size of my gut.

I had been feeling unwell all day, and that night I began having what I can only describe as contractions. Dad bundled me into the car and drove me to the emergency department. In agony, I was ordered to sit down on a hard plastic chair. The skeleton staff in the emergency department couldn't find a reason for my pain, so I was sent home. As we pulled into the driveway, doubled over in agony, I let out a primal scream. Dad turned the car around, and hours later I was finally put into a bed. X-rays of my abdomen showed I had a massive bowel obstruction. Bowel obstructions can be fatal, and when I saw my X-ray days later, it looked like there was shit rising up into my chest cavity like a smoke signal. When the bowel is in a flux of spasms, the pain is similar to contractions.

By the time I was taken up to the ward it was around 4.00 am. We had been waiting for ten hours. I was not offered pain relief.

When I woke up around 7.00 am, the head physio asked, 'What are you doing here?' I was so exhausted that I couldn't lift my head off the pillow. Over the course of the next few days, I was given a powerful laxative solution called – ironically – GoLYTELY.

Nurses tried to insert a nasogastric tube, but my nose wouldn't stop bleeding, so I tried to put one in myself. I gagged and vomited, my eyes watered, blood poured out of my nose. The next course of action was to deliver the solution rectally. In the open bathroom, I climbed up onto a bench and was rolled over on to my side. A hose was inserted into my rectum so half a litre of GoLYTELY could be emptied into my bowel. Nothing happened.

'You soaked that up like a sponge,' said one of my nurses.

The only other option was to drink the stuff and it tasted like pool water. Even when it was flavoured with cordial it still tasted bitter. A lovely doctor, whose name I'll never forget, was sitting with me in the TV room, begging me to drink. He was only a resident, and I remember hearing the tired sorrow in his voice as he sat on the side of the couch looking at the jugs of salty solution on the table in front of me.

'Please, Carly, please. You have to drink.'

I was aware that the next step involved being held down in the treatment room while a tube was forced up my nose, so I drank like my life depended on it. That day alone, I was forced to drink seven litres, and I would go on to drink twenty litres all up.

On the Monday, the matron smiled at me and said, 'If you don't eat, you don't shit, and if you don't shit, you die.'

I told her I had been eating. Then I worried about dying (again).

She looked down at my distended belly. 'Obviously.'

Eventually, the heavy-duty laxative wended its way down my large bowel. The bathroom was unisex, so while I was writhing in agony on the linoleum, any hope of privacy was dashed. Shitting yourself in a roomful of kids isn't ideal for one's sense of self.

⚘

Each year Cystic Fibrosis Queensland (CFQ) would host a camp for kids with CF and their siblings. We would go to a semi-remote location and do ridiculous activities like orienteering and canoeing – activities that, if nothing else, got us to cough up the nasty mucus that clogged our airways.

One of the campsites we used to frequent was called 'Camp Duckadang' so naturally we called it 'Fuckadang'. Camp Fuckadang had a rotunda we called a 'rootundra'. Roxette's song 'Dressed for Success' became 'Get Undressed for Oral Sex'.

One day, I was in a boat with one of my best mates, Natasha. She'd had a tough life and would, without fail, get into trouble every hospital admission. But she was one of the funniest kids I knew, and by funny, I mean gut-bustingly hilarious. There were times I literally threw up from laughter.

'I need to shit,' said Natasha.

I didn't doubt her. CF bowels could be unpredictable beasts.

'Fuck this. I can't wait. I'm gettin' in the water,' she said, as she slipped overboard.

I laughed so hard there was snot flying out of my nose and I nearly capsized the canoe. Then, all of a sudden, I could see more canoes arriving.

I started singing Salt-N-Pepa's 'Push It' – 'Ah, push it, push it real good'. I then helped her back into the canoe, where we tried to stay poker-faced as a murder of oars descended upon us.

One of our fellow campers looked into the water and gasped. 'What is that?' they asked, pointing to a log-like form floating on the surface of the water.

'Oh, I know,' another said, 'it's one of the eels they were talking about. Is that its shit?'

'Must be a fuckin' big eel,' Natasha replied, smirking at me as she dipped her oar into the water to get us back to land.

We got up to all sorts of mischief at camp. One year, someone must have forgotten to book Fuckadang because we ended up at a campsite in Hervey Bay with a bunch of very young police cadets who had been tasked with helping us with our physio and keeping us company. On the final night, they collegially shared their stash of alcohol, which my sister, Nikki, and our friend Melanie happily consumed. Someone in my group (probably Natasha) managed to procure a bottle of rum, and off we trundled into the night because our camp 'supervisors' were plastered. We were CFs and we were hardcore, and this is what we did.

After midnight, Nikki and Melanie broke into the kitchen, raided the walk-in fridge and ruined the final-day camp cake by running their fingers through the icing. The following morning the chef was not pleased.

'It must have been ... condensation,' said Nikki.

At the end of the week, there was a talent show. Natasha and I did a faux strip tease to 'Tonight' by New Kids on the Block. While it would be called inappropriate by today's standards, everyone was in full thrall. Our dance moves were overtly sexual in nature as we strolled around during the verses, then 'stripped' as the chorus broke through. If that happened now, there'd be an incident report, interviews with parents, social services, police involvement, and possibly an inquest. But it was the 1980s. The decade of decadence had not yet ended, and transgressions went conveniently unnoticed.

CF camps became a relic of the past in the early 1990s because of the risk of cross-infection. I am grateful for many things, but something I truly cherish was that I grew up when I did. Cross-infection was the death knell for hospital rooms with six-bed cubicles. For us survivors, it's a relief we didn't grow up in an isolated world. Ever since enforced isolation became de rigueur, many kids no longer know the joy of being with their kinfolk – not in person, anyway – and while they may be connected online,

online is nothing like being friends in real life. Gone are the days when we jumped into each other's beds, hugged, drank from the same cup and held kissing competitions.

I have nothing but happy memories of Natasha. We were both 'fat' CFs, and as such, copped a lot of flak for not looking emaciated. One night, back in hospital, we were watching a documentary about Elle Macpherson as we sucked on tubes of condensed milk like cigars.

'Fuck this,' I said. 'Let's go and crack some tins.'

Into the kitchen we went, searching for the big tins of condensed milk that we'd use to make caramel. We prised the cans open with a rusty can opener and glugged away. Natasha and I never did things half-arsed. She was my naughtiest friend, and every minute was an adventure.

If we had nurses on who let us run amok – which was often – I would skulk down to the chapel at night and sit quietly by myself. Other nights, I was part of a ragtag crew that would visit the adults' hospital canteen, or we went to the chapel together. There was fine gold lettering around the chapel cornices with the words: *But Jesus called them unto him, and said, 'Suffer little children, and forbid them not, to come unto me: for of such is the kingdom of God.'*

We laughed in the face of that great irony. The chapel had a small pulpit that was ideal for delivering sermons about why there was no God, or for an impromptu recitation of Sylvia Plath. It was also where we conducted the very serious business of seances. We would summon the spirits of CFs past on our rudimentary Ouija board, which was also a tradition at CF camp. Year after year, we would return to Fuckadang, inevitably down a few kids, and late at night we'd make a divine request for their presence. They rarely let us down, but let me say this: don't fuck with kids who are settled in their deadness.

When you are dying, you leak. The body reverts to primal mode where the process of ridding itself of waste begins. Surrendering grace, one oscillates between dignity and necessity. When I was dying, my simple hope was that at the end of this life, I could retain a part of who I was before my body began to rot from the inside out. When you are dying, your body does things you never expect it to. In the months leading up to my transplant, I'd already lost half of my baby-fine hair, but I didn't notice it until little tufts sprang up in the months following surgery.

By design, the body is physiologically wired to know what it needs to do during the dying process. The body expedites the draining of fluid in strange ways. For me, inactivity and the eventual inability to walk liquefied my muscles, withering the sinew and fascia until it broke down like compost – perfect textbook atrophy. I became incontinent and wet myself during coughing fits; my lips, fingers and toes were a persistent shade of blue. I coughed so violently that I vomited and farted; and I had recurrent cough syncope, teetering on the edge of consciousness. Vomiting made my eyes water and nose drip. Too much coughing can also break ribs. Broken ribs hurt. My lungs bled, and these bleeds could be perilous. And as much as I was used to seeing chunks of blood hit the bottom of the sputum cup, it was always a shock.

Bodies discharge fluids and can make enclosed spaces smell. I was familiar with the miasma of dying and death, but never before had it come from me. Life peeled away and was ladled out of me like soup. I became dissociated. Where was the girl I had shaped into a woman out of circumstance and experience? End-stage illness is not liberating, it is disempowering – akin to having your insides scooped out with a trowel and dumped into a bin. Then you are forced to crawl to said bin and shovel whatever goodness is left back into your body.

When I was dying, my world shrank: at first, it was the hospital, then the ward; then it became my hospital room, and finally my bed. At twenty-one, my world had dwindled to a mattress, my pager, sputum cups and the skyscraper of books I kept on my bedside table – the only things that got me out of the world I seemed to be trapped in. As Joan Didion once wrote, 'go to the literature'. This made more sense to me than going to the mattresses a la *The Godfather.* I was already in the mattresses, and literature – the reading and writing of it – gave me room to gather myself.

Seamus Heaney took me to the bogs and crags of his homeland, out and through The Troubles when the political became personal, and finally to a season of peace. The lull of his gentle voice soothed me at night when things went to shit – much like one of his sinking bogs.

WH Auden spirited me through the 1900s. With his epistolary and elegiac pieces, he was quite the chameleon. I never knew what I was going to get, which suited my own uncertainty.

Ted Hughes took me deep into the woods, where I met his vast bestiary. I always tried to find somewhere green in the hospital grounds to read about hares, sparrowhawks and otters, going on fox hunts and meeting Nicholas and Frieda. But Hughes had always been a peevish subject for me because of my devotion to his first wife. Sylvia Plath dragged me through motherhood, marriage and madness. Having read her poems and letters since my mid-teens, I commiserated with her flashes of neurosis because I, too, had lost my mind during the past nine months waiting to die. It felt like gestation in reverse.

⚘

While CF is often referred to as an 'invisible illness', it is never truly invisible. I was either hacking up sputum and spitting it into a cup or, at worst, swallowing great slugs of it. I always had a cough, and by cough I mean I rattled and wheezed and sounded like a machine in its death throes – which was, in part, true. There were needles that poked out of my chest, tubes that spilt from my body, and there was the oxygen I was tethered to like an astronaut on a spacewalk. There were the nasal prongs that tickled my nose and the pager on my hip to alert me should donor lungs become available.

When I was on the waiting list for my lung transplant, I found myself in a perpetual state of dizziness. I initially attributed this to my dwindling oxygen levels but then found out that the high dose of tobramycin – the IV antibiotic I was on – only added to my giddiness. It also had the potential to send me deaf. Even so, there was a new book I wanted to read before I died – *The Everlasting Story of Nory* by Nicholson Baker, so I didn't think twice about driving to Coaldrake's Bookshop in Milton to buy myself a copy. But when I got out of my car and attempted to walk the few metres uphill to collect it, my legs buckled. I sat on the footpath groping for air. I hadn't brought my oxygen tank and had to wait for a semblance of re-oxygenation before I could stand up. When I did, the long line from my port got caught under my shoe, ripping the needle out of my chest. No matter. I needed this book.

I indelicately tore the dressing off my skin, folded the oddly angled needle into itself and shoved it into my bag. It was ten minutes before I made a second attempt to reach my destination. I was bleeding from my chest, and struggled like a newborn foal as I clambered up the hill.

True to form, it turned out to be the final book I read in my unoxygenated state before I found myself on the operating table ready to have my new lungs transplanted after being on the list just short of nine months. The book was worth both the effort and the blood.

THE NIGHT I'M CALLED UP for transplant, my mum has the foresight to grab one of my university notebooks on her way out the door. From the day of my transplant until six weeks post-surgery, Mum writes detailed entries, often multiple times a day. We call them The Transplant Diaries.

Saturday 22 August 1998

12.45 am

Simon rang to tell me they had a donor for Carly. He said the ambulance was to take Carly from the Mater to the Prince Charles but that the surgery possibly wouldn't happen until 8.00 am. Carly rang us then, and Ross came and picked us up, and we all went to the Prince Charles in my car. We arrived at the hospital at about 1.30 am. Carly had just arrived, and they were wheeling her up to the ward. Then everyone started arriving – about thirty-five people. We didn't know whether Carly was going to get the lungs, but at 6.15 am, we were told yes for the go-ahead, and by 7.30, Carly was prepped for theatre.

She was calm all night because she didn't know (if the

transplant was going to happen). Finally, about 7.30, she broke down and cried on her way to theatre, realising this was it. We all said our goodbyes – 'Love you and see you soon' – and then went to wait in the Red Cross room. At 10.30, Alicia came out of theatre with her camera and said the first lung was in and inflated. She said Carly's old lungs were small and dark and shrivelled, and the new ones were lovely and pink.

By 1.30 pm, Carly's transplant doctor, Scott, came and told us that it went well, and that she was going down to ICU.

Update: we were told there was a problem. Carly has fluid around the lungs. They did an echocardiogram and found that her 'plumbing', as they call it, was too tight on an artery join as she is so small, and the donor had been larger. They had to wait for a theatre and take her back and reopen her and go back in and repair the stitching. She was still under anaesthetic, so it was good for her not having to wake up and then be told she had to go back to theatre. It was so emotional seeing her ventilated, with tubes and drips everywhere. She came back at 6.15 pm Saturday night, and her surgeon, Doctor Tam, said that all was okay. She has a sign up beside her bed saying, 'Hi Carly! You made it!'

When I'm on life support, my body resembles a human wishbone. On day four, I am awake and breathing on my own – in part. In part, because I'm breathing with another person's lungs. Where I should feel elated, I'm in such a stupor of pain that I want to know how the nurses let a lunatic into intensive care to pour fuel over my chest and drop a lit match. It isn't just my chest burning – it is as if my soul is aflame. But when I look down, all I see are four hoses poking out just beneath my breasts. Later, I will allegorise this searing pain as the husk of my old body falling away;

like a slipping of skins and the exquisite agony of being caught between being a girl and a woman.

⸸

For anyone following my story, it might look like I've been smashed against the grindstone of life. Life was a carolling of joy, then a smack of despair, yet I was deeply in love with my life as a kid. I had an incredible group of friends, and I loved school and everything that came with it. I always loved to sing. Mum says I used to poke my head through the fence railings to perform for our elderly neighbours. Living in a cul-de-sac proved to be my very own theatre, and I would stroll around singing for hours. Not singing to anyone in particular – just the whole street.

'You were full of spunk – always singing and dancing, always joking around.'

I had been doing jazz and tap classes at The Ritz Dancing School since I was six years old. I was ten when I was chosen to participate in a weekend dance intensive with some of Brisbane's best dancers. In my black and white leotard, I was in the zone and having the time of my life, but Missy Rhonda, my dance teacher, was petrified that I was going to get heat stroke. We were, after all, wrapped in a foul Brisbane summer.

As well as dancing, I arched and bent myself into a pretzel at gymnastics, sang in the choir and was one of eight students in vocal group, where we swept the awards at school eisteddfods. In primary school every year there was a Christmas concert, and in grade one, in front of a few hundred people, I asked if I could sing. Every Christmas after that, the principal, Mr Kelly, would shout out, 'Where's Carly?' He would hand me the microphone; I'd leap on stage and lead the crowd in Christmas carols.

'You were fearless. You'd get hold of the microphone, and

you'd lead the band. I have no idea where that came from,' says Mum.

In my senior year, I landed the role of a femme fatale in *Bugsy Malone* where I got to sing a big number while wearing suspenders as I straddled a chair, with the nuns from my school in the front row, spines rigid in their chairs, and owl-eyed. The day after opening night, I was at school when I started coughing up blood. Mum drove me to hospital where I was given a vitamin K injection (vitamin K helps blood coagulate), and I went on to belt out 'The Man I Love' that night, sultrily but with my usual power. After I exited the stage, one of the younger boys came up to me.

'I don't think you were as good as opening night.'

I flicked my feather boa over my shoulder and smiled. I thought to myself, *That's because I've been coughing up blood, you little prick.*

On the final night, my grandmother came to the show and couldn't believe that it was me singing. 'That was you?'

'Yeah!'

'No, it wasn't!'

'Nana, it was me.'

I was never one to rehearse at home, and when I did sing and had the house to myself, she would be up the other end in her granny flat.

'I thought it was a recording, love!'

I giggled and pulled her in for a hug.

'I mean, I knew you could belt it out, but my god!'

The musicals were the highlight of my entire high school experience. It was a time where my voice would unspool from my body with an unseen urgency. One day in rehearsals, the music teacher at another school who played in a well-known Brisbane jazz band asked me if I'd like to be their front woman of a weekend. I was shocked to be asked, and while every cell of my being screamed 'yes', with schoolwork, regular infections and hospitalisations, I knew I had to decline.

'Oh my god, can you imagine?' I said to Mum.

'It would be amazing. You would be amazing.'

'But it would ruin me,' I said, and as Mum turned away, I knew she was crying.

I didn't tell anyone at school. No-one likes a braggart. Instead, I doubled back to that familiar place of radical acceptance. I didn't tell anyone I had an acting agent, either. All I had wanted to do my whole life was sing and act, and I'd been given a massive – and unexpected – opportunity. But I knew the trajectory of my disease. I wasn't going to get better.

After my transplant, my new lungs never feel like they shouldn't be there. At the intersection of illness, each experience is like a fingerprint – there are no two outcomes or experiences the same. Each has their own topography and rejects any kind of homogeneity. Every person and every body reacts differently.

The experience of grief and loss related to a lost body part or organ is often ignored in mainstream medical and health culture. In fact, limbs and organs that are removed are usually disposed of under a veil of impersonal darkness, with little or no acknowledgement. I know that my 'native' lungs ended up in a plastic bucket, then were taken to a lab for research. Losing a body part or organ can be the cause of great psychological trauma. No-one talks about what it will feel like post-transplant because we are hyper-focused on survival. For some recipients, we integrate our new bodily form into a sense of meaningfulness, allowing us to farewell what has been lost. My friend Natasha found it impossible to wrap her head around the fact that she had someone else's organs inside her. She wanted to purge them from the outset, and she died a dislocated soul – scared to live – only finding peace in death.

I am in hospital when Natasha dies. I write:

12 February 2004

11.25 am

A knot. Me in one room, all pink and angry and alive, a childhood friend in another room – blue and angry and on the end-pitch of not being here at all. Grew up with her. We misbehaved together and fed off each other's imperfections and repertoire of smut. We grieved together; held each other through funerals, got drunk on Passion Pop and rum, found a bag of weed at a party and smoked it. Always the healthier of the two (and the four – Natasha, Meagan, Wendy and me), she clamours for breath and snarls at things we cannot see, like the ghost of her boyfriend who hung himself and the spirits of friends that have come to try and calm her. Rattling on a morphine cloud that's not really taking her anywhere, she bucks on the metal bed like a tethered animal not used to captivity. She bangs on walls out of fear with her fists, while I sit on my bed of steel with its crude mattress. I breathe. This freedom of breath seems selfish. I can carve a road to dark passages with a full belly and a heaving chest of air, but she is caught in that death-trap of a bed, banging on the wall. Why be it this way?

⚘

I have a knack for opening jars of memories, but these moments are often trapped within an eternal present, and I can't reconfigure them into a memory because they are so pervasive. Among my first is being behind bars. It takes me years to iron out that this would have been me in a cot when I was in hospital as a baby. Another early memory is of the gusts of wind that would barrel up the hill and roar through the trees at our first house. The eucalypts would gracefully lean into each other, shirring the air, and were especially powerful during a bitter westerly. People talk about their earliest memories – about sleepovers at their grandparents, playing with a particular friend or a toy – and while I do remember these things, my most pervasive memories are the ones where I'm being repeatedly punctured with needles, being slapped on my tender trunk during physio, wanting to talk to my mum when I was upset and alone in hospital, as well as a host of other instances that are undeniably abnormal for a child. But it was normal for me, and so I learnt to master the art of adaptation. I was inhumanly proficient at it. Like water passing over a river stone, CF whittled me into the person I would go on to become.

⚘

I was around six when Mum told me about sex. I remember my sister had a friend over, and Mum took me upstairs to tell me about the basics. After our very open chat, I ran to my sister and her friend, spilt the beans and got a smack on the backside for my trouble. Mum was always happy to answer any questions I had, took my sister and I to stranger danger classes (what we called PE – pervert education), and told me that should anyone touch me in a way I didn't like, I needed to let her know.

Dad, on the other hand, was very strict. By no means was he a prude, but when it came to my sister and me, he was dubious about the intentions of every boy and would tell them so.

'Why are you so paranoid?' I would ask.

'I was their age once.'

'That's not exactly encouraging.'

'That's not what I mean, love.'

As a young teenager, when I reached into my underpants, I was always disappointed by my lack of pubic hair. Would I ever grow more than three strands? Why were they so blonde? Wasn't pubic hair supposed to be black? From what I had seen (the joys of an all-girls school), all of my friends' pubic hair was dark and curly. Was CF stunting my pubic hair and breast growth? Was all the physio I had on my chest the reason I had mosquito bites for boobs? And where was my period?

When I was getting ready to go to my first school dance, Dad took me aside and read me the riot act: 'No kissing, no necking, *nothing*.'

Necking? Was that something they did in the fifties? If all went according to plan, I was going to be PASHING.

'I *mean* it, Carly,' he said, pointing his finger at me as though that held some weight.

Dad had volunteered to be on 'parent patrol', so with his police-issue Maglite torch that could crush a young boy's skull, I estimate he crossed the hall dozens of times that night.

It was at this first dance I had my first real kiss. As the dulcet tones of EMF's 'Unbelievable' were sweeping over hundreds of sweaty, hormonal teenagers, I found myself in a groove with a stunner of a boy who had lovely dark brown, floppy hair. A group of kids pushed past us and nearly knocked me over, and the boy with the floppy hair picked me up and kissed me. His name was Nathaniel.

Okay, I thought. *So, this is life.*

⚘

When I was sixteen, I met the love of my life. Or at least, my sixteen-year-old brain and body thought I had met the love of my life. In 1993, the private girls school I attended had just finished a three-night show of the musical *Pirates of Penzance* where I was cast in a principal role. We had done the musical with one of the private boys schools. Adrian was the best-looking boy in grade eleven, and on our first parent-free date, it felt like we'd just left prison after years of being in the hole. He lived quite a distance from my house and the hospital, but he still took the time to visit and while away the hours with me.

I had my own room at the end of the ward where no-one disturbed me unless it was for physio or to hook me up for my IV. By now, I couldn't give a flying fuck about whether I had pubic hair or not, and Adrian was adept at slipping his hand into my underwear.

One day he was there when I needed to access my port. A port-a-cath, or port, is a small, round disc made of plastic or metal that is surgically placed under the skin. A catheter connects the port to an artery – usually your subclavian, which lies under your collarbone. The port has a septum so medications like intravenous antibiotics, chemotherapy or blood products can be administered. Adrian was standing behind me and seemed most pleased when I whipped off my shirt to reveal a lacy black bra. Lust turned to alarm, however, when he saw that I'd grabbed a needle and was pushing it through my skin. He collapsed on my bed saying, 'Oh fuck. Oh FUCK!'

I turned around, still pushing the needle into my chest. 'It's really no big deal, babe.' Being independent made me feel like I had some semblance of control, so I had been accessing my own port since I was twelve. Sticking needles into my groin and chest was all very normal for me. Drawing back the plunger and seeing the flash of blood was like a reckoning, the plastic warm in my hand as it filled with blood. If a warm gun was happiness for The Beatles, a warm flash of blood was mine.

The port – as I saw it – had become part of my body, and

it made life easier. The septum, made of a self-sealing silicone, could be punctured thousands of times before it needed replacing. To administer intravenous drugs, the skin over the port was disinfected, then it was accessed by puncturing the skin with a right-angled needle, which looked much like an Allen key. But they could be pernickety. Having a port could make being a passenger in a car uncomfortable. Seatbelts always had a knack for pushing the needle further into my chest when the car came to a very sudden stop, and I would feel the needle hit the base of the port with a dull 'thud'.

One winter's afternoon, Adrian and I fell asleep in my hospital bed. It was a school night, and at first his parents thought he'd wagged the last couple of periods of school to come and see me. But when he didn't come home, his mother became frantic, his father, apoplectic. They called my parents to no avail, then drove all the way to the hospital to find us asleep.

I'd never been so blissed out in my life, but his parents were not impressed. As Adrian left he tried not to rouse me. I sensed him getting up and half-opened my eyes.

'Go back to sleep, baby. I love you,' he whispered.

'I love you, too,' I mumbled, and fell back to sleep.

I fail to remember if I got a talking-to because I was floating on a cloud of love and lust where nothing and no-one could touch me. We wrote each other love letters, and in one he wrote that he wanted me to be his wife. *This is it*, I thought. *I've met the person I'm going to marry and hopefully have a family with.* But having a sick girlfriend became too much for him, and we broke up. I was bereft and cried all the time. If Dad so much as looked at me the wrong way, I burst into tears.

'But I didn't *say* anything!' he'd say to my mum, throwing his hands in the air.

Not long after this, I decided that having a life-limiting illness, studying for my HSC, witnessing suffering and death on a grand scale, and dealing with boys felt oppressive. And sex? That was more responsibility than I was interested in having, despite having earned the nickname 'the sex goddess' in high school.

That same year, I finally got my period and immediately regretted willing it to happen. Every month, my body was concertinaed in pain with what felt like a gallon of blood in my belly. I was referred to a gynaecologist who ordered some tests, one of which included an internal ultrasound. That is how I found myself in a dark room one afternoon with a middle-aged sonographer and my mum.

'Would you like your mum to stay?'

'It's okay – she doesn't need to see this. That would just be cruel.' I laughed.

When the sonographer pulled a condom out of its packet, calling it a 'medical sheath' in a camp voice to rival Tim Curry, it dissipated any tension. I never thought this would be my first encounter with a condom. Then I saw the probe he picked up.

'That?!'

'Listen, I know it looks like the big kahuna – and it is – but you're going to be fine. I'll take you through step by step, I promise.'

It looked like a baseball bat. Once I put the 'medical sheath' on I took the probe and guided it into my vagina. The sonographer showed me the shadows on the screen and told me what they meant – where my uterus was, where my ovaries were, and where the endometrial lining had grown outside my womb. It was very entertaining, and after about twenty minutes, we were done.

'How're you feeling?' Mum asked me on the way home.

'I'm fine.'

'Good stuff.'

'Even though I just lost my virginity to an ultrasound probe.'

I was diagnosed with endometriosis, and despite my

gynaecologist putting me on the contraceptive pill to lessen the bleeding and the pain, by the time I was seventeen I needed surgery. At this point, the most terrifying surgery I'd experienced was my third port insertion. In that instance, what should have been a minor surgery turned out to be chilling. When the anaesthetist administered the paralytics to disable my respiratory system, it rendered me unable to breathe on my own. I'd been conscious as I listened to him talk about his golf handicap, but as hard as I tried, I couldn't breathe or scream or blink an eye to let anyone know. I remember being surprised to wake up in recovery, because I was certain I was going to die.

Because of this earlier experience, I was terrified by the idea of another surgery. When I explained my concerns, the surgeon told me about these wonderful things called pre-meds. I don't remember a lot after I changed into a purple gown and swallowed some tiny pills, but while pre-meds would quell my pre-surgical anxiety, endometriosis would prove to be an ongoing adversary.

Mum had once warned me that, 'Your first love is your worst love', but for me it was my second love that made the biggest impression.

In 1991, when I was fourteen, my lungs tested positive for the superbug MRSA (multi-resistant staph aureus). I walked back to the ward from school one afternoon and found all of my belongings on my bed in preparation to be taken to Patterson Ward – the ward for infectious diseases. Patterson Ward was in a primitive demountable while the new children's hospital was being built. The upside was that it had single rooms, which were big enough for me to practise my cello and meant my friends and I could hang out in private. When we moved from the demountable to the new hospital, each of the six floors had a colour and Patterson's was pink. Everything was decorated in varying shades of salmon – from the chairs to the walls to the curtains, even the lino.

I was in and out of the hospital for the next few years. By 1994, the MRSA in my lungs mercifully disappeared, and I finally returned to Robertson Ward, where everything from the floor to the ceiling was blue. It was there that I met Marcelo for the second time. I remembered him distinctly from a few years earlier because male nursing students were such a rarity, and all the female nurses were aflutter with his kind and gentle manner. His brilliant smile and body, which was akin to a modern-day Adonis (white uniforms made it easy to see the topography of one's body), meant that he got a lot of attention on the ward. The first time we crossed paths, we were both standing in the creaky elevator when I got the giggles.

'Sorry,' I said.

'That's okay,' he replied. He smiled as he exited the lift. I may only have been fourteen, but I made a mental note of his peachy arse.

When I am seventeen, and find myself back in Robertson Ward with yet another chest infection, I am excited to see my favourite night nurse, Sue. I had stayed up late to see her and I walked into the treatment room where she and Marcelo were drawing up drugs for our 11.00 pm IVs. I was wearing a little silk slip dress and thought nothing of jumping up on the bed to chat away to them while they worked. I found out that Marcelo only worked night duty, and when he smiled at me, I wanted to disappear. Not because it was strange, but because it made me feel like I was about to melt into a puddle of something I couldn't quite describe.

When my friends visited late one night, they understood why I talked about him so much at school.

'Why is he a nurse, anyway?'

'What do you mean?' I asked, in my opioid haze.

'Why isn't he a model?' they asked.

'I have no idea, but I do know that I'm totally going to marry him.'

'Yeah, Carls – in your dreams,' they responded, howling with laughter.

Through the course of that year, Marcelo and I got to know each other. There was no doubt in my mind that I was falling in love, but I was still just a freckled seventeen-year-old, my most redeeming features being a summer tan and blonde hair that fell to my hips. Why would the most beautiful man in the world have given me a second thought?

Not long after I finished high school, my friend Steph drove me down to the Gold Coast in her convertible four-wheel drive. We were going to visit Marcelo on surf lifesaving duty. I nearly fainted when I saw him in his swimmers because I'd only ever seen him in his white uniform. 'Palm Beach' was splayed in capital letters across that perfect arse.

I frolicked in the water in my tiny blue string bikini, my long hair slicked all the way down my back as I walked in from the dumpers. After a couple of hours on the beach, Steph drove us back to Marcelo's house where he and I sat together on his bed, talking. He gave me a card for my upcoming birthday on New Year's Eve, with the words: *The gem cannot be polished without friction, nor people perfected without trials – Chinese Proverb. To a dear, dear friend, have a very happy birthday and may life give you whatever you seek from it and more. Love always, Marcelo.*

The three of us went back to my place. I was not expecting him to get out of the car, so I was surprised when he gave me a hug. He said, 'I'd really love to do this again', which gave me a flash of 'What if?'

We continued to talk on the phone, and two days before my eighteenth birthday he packed a picnic, and we wended our way up into the Gold Coast hinterland. In the car, I noticed his thick arms twitching with muscle as he changed gears, and I couldn't work out why I was feeling so nervous. As we packed up lunch, he looked at me with his searing brown eyes, but I failed to hold his gaze, because I was worried he was going to tell me something I didn't want to hear. And, in a way, he did.

'I thought I'd better tell you that I've transferred from Robertson Ward to the Intensive Care Unit,' he said.

'Why?' I asked.

After a few beats of silence, with sudden clarity I knew what he was about to say. Ever so gently, he told me that he wanted to be more than friends. My face flushed, I put half an avocado into a Tupperware container and said, 'Oh.' My brain short-circuited. I tried to speak, but I was speechless. Looking back, I can only imagine how nervous he would have been. He had put his entire career on the line in that moment.

Once I came back into my body, I said, 'I'd really love that.'

'Really?' he asked, flashing me one of his heart-melting smiles, as though he'd been preparing himself for me to say I wasn't interested. We packed up the picnic and walked back to his car, hand in hand. He pulled me into a massive hug and kissed my forehead, and then we drove from the mountain to the beach. Our first kiss exploded like diamonds across the water. We held hands all the way back to Brisbane and wouldn't let go of each other for months.

But still the question remained – why would I be on his radar when he could be with any woman he wanted? Later, Marcelo would tell me that he fell in love with my kindness and ferocity. He hated the feeling of powerlessness when he saw me devastated at the funerals of other CF kids. He would say how he wanted to wrap me up so he could protect me from the pain.

My eighteenth birthday was the best day of my life so far. I was with a man I'd loved from afar for so long, and my auntie and uncle, visiting from Perth, sent me off on a Harley-Davidson ride across the city. We blasted our way to Marcelo's house, but he wasn't there because he was waiting nervously at my house with a bunch of flowers. When we pulled into the driveway, I saw relief painted across his face, and I couldn't work out why. He told me later that he had been in a motorcycle accident years before and was having a panic attack about me being in a crash. That night – New Year's Eve – my family and I went out to dinner and celebrated the milestone that I'd made it to adulthood. I looked at Marcelo for most of the night, marvelling at his beauty and his gentlemanly gestures. He would stand up when I did, pulled the chair out for me, and wasn't afraid of showing his affection. It occurred to me that this was the first real man I had ever been with.

As with all the patients at the kid's hospital, when I turned eighteen, it was time to transition to the adults' ward. My relationship with Marcelo was also proving to be the subject of much consternation inside the hospital. Put simply, there were some nurses who couldn't cope with the fact that Marcelo had chosen to be with me. One day, when I was about to go on day leave, a nurse who had taken particular umbrage to our relationship wouldn't let me leave the treatment room. She closed the door, pinned me against it and asked where I was going.

'Out,' I explained.

'Is he picking you up?' she asked.

'Yes.'

'You know you need permission from a parent, don't you?'

'I'm eighteen. I'm going now.'

'No, you're not.'

'Yes, I am.'

'I'll get the wardies onto you.'

'Okay. Still leaving.'

I extricated myself from the room and walked at speed down the hall, knowing that Marcelo was waiting for me downstairs.

'Carly!' she called out after me.

I ran into one of my favourite wardies in the hall, and there was no way he was going to stop me from leaving. These guys were protective of us CFs and would have put themselves between me and anyone giving me trouble.

'Hey Lloyd!'

'G'day Carly!'

'Have an awesome day, mate.'

'You too, darl!'

I dashed out of the hospital and jumped into Marcelo's car.

'Quick – go!'

'What's wrong?' he asked, speeding away.

'Astrid just tried to stop me from leaving the ward.'

'She what?'

I told him what had just transpired.

'She threatened to get the wardies to stop me.'

'Good luck with that.'

Marcelo pulled onto the side of the road so we could share a hello kiss. These kisses were the best.

'Hi,' I whispered, with a ridiculous grin.

'I love you,' he said, as he ran his hands through my hair.

'I love you, too. Let's get out of here.'

That afternoon, my friend Kate and I caught up at each other's beds.

'What happened this morning? Astrid was rank!'

I told her the story.

'Fucking psychopath. She only hates you because she's a fat moll who has the hots for Marcelo.'

'There may be an element of truth in that,' I said, and we both had a giggle.

The next run-in was a few days later. I was sitting on Kate's bed while Astrid and another nurse fished our medication out of a stainless-steel trolley.

'Carly, why are you on Nilstat?'

'Here we go,' I whispered to Kate. 'Why do you think I'm on Nilstat, Astrid?'

'Because you have thrush.'

'That's right.'

'Does Marcelo know?'

'I don't know, Astrid. Kate – does Marcelo know I have THRUSH?'

'Yes Carly. He found it with his tongue,' she said, as though reporting a very important story on the six o'clock news.

I was rolling around on the bed having a coughing fit from laughter. I wasn't expecting this welcome vulgarity so early in the morning, but Kate was quick and very witty. The room erupted into laughter, and it was easy to see the other nurse was embarrassed by Astrid's line of questioning.

'Anything else about my sex life?' I asked.

'Carly! You have a sex life with hot-as-fuck nurse Marcelo?' asked Kate in mock disgust.

It wasn't long after that I shipped myself off to the Mater Adults in South Brisbane. Marcelo took me to my new second home, where I was packed into a room with three elderly women. He helped me get settled, and when he left, we were both in tears. We hugged for the longest time.

'It's okay,' I said.

'No, it's not. I don't want to leave you here,' he said.

It proved to be a strange night. I didn't know anyone, but the nurses were friendly, and I had full confidence in my new doctor because he had come highly recommended by the fussiest person I knew – my friend Michelle. I cried all night.

The next morning, someone shat the bed just as breakfast arrived. Moving to the adults' hospital was a baptism by shit. There was no 'transition'. One day I was in the children's hospital, and the next I was in a four-bed cubicle with patients who often had dementia. That in itself was fine, but when I was sharing a room with geriatric men, I would often walk to the bathroom only to find the toilet floor swimming in piss. I lost count of the number of times I was asked for a bedpan because – being the youngest patient on the ward – the other patients assumed I was a nurse. I would help the older ladies out of bed and put up their bed rails so they didn't roll onto the floor in the night. I cut up their food and helped them eat when the ward was short-staffed.

And so, I had gone from nursing the young to looking after the elderly, again noticing how stark the bookends of life were. These women, once grand dames and fierce matriarchs, had outlived their families and were usually waiting for placement in a nursing home. It was terribly sad, but I had a lot of affection for older people, which made the change a little easier to bear.

During this time, when we were in the full throat of our love, Marcelo and I couldn't bear to be away from each other. When I wasn't in hospital, my parents let him stay the night, but he had to sleep on cushions on the floor where we held hands until we both fell asleep. At his place, we walked around naked, ate juicy stone fruit naked, played naked backgammon and had baths together. His body would hold mine like a canoe, and I nestled him between my legs as I washed down his chiselled torso. Marcelo was in between my legs a lot. We navigated the topology of each other's bodies, and he learnt every millimetre of my flesh. I had my first orgasm to Bach, and it was so intense that I fell off the bed. Every day we didn't see each other was like a little hell. We both felt like we were missing a limb. In April, we went away to a secluded cabin in the hinterland, where I arrived as a girl on the cusp of womanhood and left as a fully-fledged sexual being. We wrote each other reams of love letters and poems and for a while, everything felt perfect. We were unbreakable.

In February 1996, my friend Michelle died in an intensive care unit, and the next day my grandmother died of cancer. In the same hospital. Later that month came another death when I broke off my relationship with Marcelo for the final time. Three deaths, and we were only into the second month of the year.

My earliest memory of Michelle is being in a bed next to her in Adelaide Billing. She was wearing an oxygen mask and yelling at her mother on the ward phone while shaving her legs with an electric razor.

Michelle was a cyclone, which both enchanted and terrified me. Whip-smart, she was studying computer science at university and, like me, always had books on the trolley next to her bed. We spent a fair bit of time in hospital together until she got a call in 1991 – a heart and lungs were available for her in Sydney. She was so sick at the time that her boyfriend, Paul, had to carry her everywhere. By the time Mum, Dad, Nikki and I saw her off at the airport, she had whittled down to the size of a sparrow.

Michelle did well for a few years post-transplant, but by the time I got together with Marcelo, she was having problems with cancerous cells in her cervix, likely caused by the heavy immunosuppression she was on. She recovered, but then she got a lung infection. In the weeks preceding her death, I would take her up some soup (forever known as 'Michelle's soup') and sit with her. Only a year earlier, she had asked me to be her bridesmaid – she was due to marry Paul in April. The day she took me fabric shopping she arrived in their red RX7. In the January heat, the rotary engine had overheated and after a few failed attempts, Marcelo managed to get the car started, and off we cackled into the sunset.

On 10 February, her sister called me and told me that I needed to get to the hospital to talk some sense into her.

'She's not listening to anyone. She might listen to you.'

When I walked into her room, it was abundantly clear – at least to me – that something was dreadfully wrong. Michelle didn't need a talking-to – she was struggling to breathe and was barely conscious. I took her hand and told her how much she had to live for, and that I loved her. After leaving her room, I talked with her sister and Paul about what was happening. I left the hospital but couldn't shake the feeling that I needed to be with her. I drove back, and when I arrived, around 7.30 pm, I met a couple of their friends in the hospital lobby. They let me know Michelle was being taken down for an X-ray. Everyone was scattered, oscillating between 'It's going to be okay' to 'What the fuck is going on?' I rushed up to the ward to make sure I was there when her bed was moved to the medical imaging department.

A group of us followed Michelle's bed to the imaging room. Within a couple of minutes, a code blue rang out over the hospital PA system. We looked at each other and made the horrific connection that this was the room Michelle was in. A group of doctors sprinted down the hall on their way to resuscitate her, while I ran to get her dad. As I ran, for some reason, I yelled, 'She's that way.'

After a time, a doctor who had a reputation for being gruff emerged from the quiet of the darkened room to tell us that

Michelle had gone into cardiac arrest. He went on to say that despite working on her for twenty minutes, she was brain dead. A switch had been flicked and her light extinguished, even though her heart was still beating. He explained that she was on life support and would be taken up to ICU, and that we should call the relevant people. This was a doctor who throughout his career had given the worst news to hundreds of families, and in that moment, I was struck that he broke it to us with inordinate kindness. Then, as if we were in an episode of a soap opera, Michelle's father collapsed and was rushed around the corner to emergency with a suspected heart attack. I immediately thought of takotsubo cardiomyopathy – broken heart syndrome.

We were mired in shock. Knowing there was nothing that could be done for Michelle, I called my family and Marcelo telling them what had happened. After Michelle was settled into ICU, I walked downstairs to see my grandmother, who, herself, was between worlds. I must have looked bleary-eyed because when I walked into the ward to check what room Nana was in, the nurse looked at me and asked if I was alright. In a far-off voice that didn't feel like mine, I told her I was fine.

'Are you sure?'

I nodded like an automaton.

I held my grandmother's hand and whispered how much I loved her and how much it had meant having her in my life. Knowing what was coming, I asked her to look after Michelle. I watched over her for what seemed like the longest time, kissed her cool, papery skin, and left. That would be the last time I saw her.

When I arrived back at ICU, Marcelo was there. Of course he was. We sat on the floor of the quiet, carpeted hallway holding hands, stunned into silence. It was as if my jaw had locked shut. There were no words. There was no sound. Soon, we were asked if we would like to go and spend some time with our friend. Like anyone entering intensive care for the first time, everything was foreign and overwhelming. Michelle didn't look like herself. For starters, she was silent. Michelle was never silent. She had a tube down her throat that was keeping her heart and lungs working, and her face was puffy because her kidneys were beginning to shut down. When the time came to withdraw life support, we were all touching a part of her. I was holding on to one of her feet. She fucking hated being touched on her feet.

When life support is withdrawn, the doctors don't actually 'pull the plug'. It was gentle and silent – almost as though it wasn't happening. The rhythm of Michelle's heart on the monitor never completely flatlined because she had a pacemaker, and Paul was distressed that he could still see his fiancée's heart beating. Her heart had stopped, but he was panicked, as anyone unfamiliar with the endless rhythm of a pacemaker would be. It was 4.05 am on Sunday 11 February. Michelle was dead.

The next day, my grandmother died.

On Tuesday, the universe offered us a day of grace. Wednesday was Valentine's Day and Michelle's funeral. Marcelo gave me a diamond ring, and we drove to Michelle's alma mater, Star of the Sea. I had been asked to do a reading at her service, and at her wake strangers approached me to ask if I was Michelle's sister because of our husky voices. I got messily drunk and ended up in a bed with Paul and our friend Gavin. It sounds far more sordid than it actually was. Everyone was plastered. We were grieving and celebrating Michelle, which was a confusing combination, and while there was nothing to it, Marcelo wasn't happy. The next day, we farewelled my grandmother. I spoke at her service, got very, very drunk again and ended the afternoon with my legs wrapped around Marcelo's head, dissolving into desire.

A couple of weeks after we buried Michelle, I was rundown and needed to be admitted to hospital for a lung infection. Later that evening, it registered that I was in the same room Michelle had been in just before she died. The same room I had seen her struggling for breath in. Heavy with premonition, I cried for most of the night, yet there was also a sense of comfort. I knew her spirit wasn't lingering between worlds, but there was a sensation I couldn't put a name to. It was a rich and strange feeling, and not entirely unfamiliar, because it was something I'd felt before. It was something I had felt on and off my whole life.

Spirituality has been a thread spooling through my life. I know I'm uniquely connected to things, feelings and people in ways I can't explain. Growing up, there were frequent occurrences where I felt a presence around me, and often not just one presence, but multiple. I had my first supernatural experience when I was six years old. I knew my friend Rachel was very sick and that she wasn't going to get better. One morning, I told Mum that I'd had a dream about her.

'What happened?' Mum asked.

'She floated through my window, sat on my bed and said she had to go and that she wanted to say goodbye.'

Mum had received a call that morning letting her know that Rachel had died overnight.

'I don't think that was a dream, darling,' she said, and I knew exactly what she meant. I'm fortunate to have parents who didn't push this part of me down.

There were times in the dying room when things happened that I couldn't explain. The lights in the wall above the two beds would often flicker on and off. I lost count of the number of times the hospital electrician was called to replace globes and check wiring, but the flickering lights persisted. My friend Kate felt it too. The lights were especially erratic when we were talking about our dead friends. We'd look at each other in this creepy two-bed room and say, 'Fuck – did you see/hear/smell that?' Of course we did. We would describe the same thing, word for word.

Before us CFs colonised Adelaide Billing Ward, it wasn't uncommon for nurses to put unsettled babies into the smaller room on night shift. On many occasions, nurses would walk in to find the cot rail down and a baby in a deep sleep. We believed it was Matron Billing keeping vigil over them. It was never broached that it could be a practical joke. Nurses would never leave a cot rail down. There were stories about burettes being filled, blankets and toys being rearranged. Even in death, Matron Billing was greatly loved and respected. And yet, there was always an undercurrent of darkness to Adelaide Billing, and there was one part of the ward, in particular, that terrified me. It was the fire escape at the back of the TV room where a disused ping pong table and decommissioned beds and cots were kept. I can't remember a single time I approached that fire escape without feeling like the air had been sucked out of the room.

One night, a male nurse found her filling a burette, and while he thought her face looked vaguely familiar, it wasn't until he saw a photo of Matron Billing hanging in the foyer that he knew he'd seen a ghost.

She was often seen ambling down the halls at night, making sure her charges were comfortable, stroking foreheads, tucking in bedclothes, straightening pillows. These quiet stories were passed down from nurses of the old guard, and they were kept quiet for a reason. These women – in the fraternal halls of medicine – didn't want to be seen as being mad.

The thing with these rich and strange encounters, spiritual or otherwise, is that they've been so deeply stigmatised, pilloried and invalidated that no-one wants to speak freely about them unless it's with someone they trust. I think about Adelaide Billing most days – the ward where I spent so much of my childhood features in my dreams every couple of weeks, sloping terrazzo buttressed against the walls, heavy-set doors and the ancient elevator that would lurch from floor to floor.

⚘

I knew Marcelo wanted to marry me, and for a while, both the thought and the feeling were thrilling. I couldn't remember ever being this happy. But after falling so deeply in love, I also wanted my freedom, especially when my friends' eighteenth birthdays started to fall in quick succession, and I had a desire to go out and experience the world. We'd broken up a couple of times in the past few months. On my nineteenth birthday we were apart – me on Stradbroke Island, him celebrating New Year's Eve at The Wickham in Fortitude Valley.

It was hard to reconcile the disconnect from our feelings of only a year before. We reunited briefly in the new year, but when Michelle died, we died. My grief wouldn't let me love him. I needed to be alone. I was numb with sorrow; I didn't want to be loved or touched. Instead, I spent most of my weekends trying to douse my devastation in alcohol. I later joked that I was drunk for six months, but there's an element of truth in that. Thanks to my perfectionist complex, I was also studying full-time, determined to get a perfect GPA.

Marcelo and I bumped into each other a few years after my transplant. His face was wrapped into a huge smile as he approached me with a baby boy strapped to his chest, and I could feel his trademark warmth when he told me how happy he was that I had done so well. In the years after this, I tried to contact him, but had to face one simple fact – I'd broken his heart. We had our life together mapped out and were each other's world until I jumped off our axis. One day, I would like to tell him face to face how sorry I am, instead of crying out those words into the void – I'm sorry. I am so, so sorry that I hurt you. He was the kindest, most pure-hearted soul I would ever meet. I can only hope I was his favourite mistake.

It used to terrify me that he might never give me so much as a second thought. I was his Lolita, biblically and primitively pure. We cut our teeth on summer and shed our winter skins together. He was my education, and I was his lesson. I physically ache when I cast my mind back to when he would wash my long hair with such tenderness and devotion. Having my hair washed was one of the most romantic and sexiest things anyone has ever done for me. I loved him with my whole self, and each part of my flesh was his. I might have woken in a world of pain when I slept on his futon, but it was worth it because it meant being held by him all night. Dad has asked me over the years if I regret that I broke it off with Marcelo.

'I can't. I wouldn't have been able to give him children. He wouldn't have had the career that he's had.'

'I don't think he would have minded, love. As long as he was with you. I've never seen a person so devoted to another.'

'You know what? He was the love of my life, and I think I'm lucky I even got to experience love like that. Not everyone gets to love like we did.'

Sometimes, I drive past his old house. I often think about knocking on the door, but what would I say?

'Hi! I had my first orgasm here. Mind if I have a look through? Love what you've done with the place.'

To the public, doctors have been seen as sacrosanct, especially surgeons. Reliable, trustworthy, infallible, and worryingly – untouchable. But they are human and make mistakes, and when you literally hold a person's life in your gloved hands, making a mistake should not be easy to come back from. In 1996, when I was nineteen, my fourth port was incorrectly placed in my groin. Doctors used image intensifiers to access it with needles that were two and three inches long, but they still couldn't penetrate the septum. After a couple of weeks, with a three-inch needle hanging out of my groin, I asked that it be removed, and my parents paid for a private vascular surgeon. He visited that afternoon to tell us that the port had been inserted back to front – doctors had been trying to pierce stainless steel.

'How the hell did that happen?' asked my dad.

'Maybe they were sucking on the nitrous oxide in theatre,' I joked.

'It's unfortunate, and you should perhaps consider a lawsuit,' said the vascular surgeon.

After he left, Dad said, 'I could have put that in the right way up after twenty-five beers.'

Of course, we didn't proceed with a lawsuit, because you don't want to bite the hand that feeds you. Also, it wouldn't have changed anything. A few weeks later, it was replaced by a fifth port in my chest. Then I had a sixth. Mercifully, both were placed correctly.

⚘

As the lung transplant surgical team mill around me in theatre before they pump me full of propofol, I ask, 'So, what are the chances of a couple of 500 mil bags of normal saline finding their way into my chest right where my boobs are?'

They laugh. 'You're not the first woman to ask that.' It seems to defuse the tension.

'I doubt I'll be the last.'

When I'm on life support in ICU after my lung transplant, a young intensivist strides into my ICU pod to remove my sixth port. Anything 'foreign' poses an infection risk due to high levels of immunosuppression, and this includes ports and breast implants.

And so, the port must come out.

'I'll have this out in twenty minutes,' the doctor says to my parents.

Mum nods politely because she knows it won't be as easy as he thinks. What he hadn't counted on is the labyrinthine scar tissue and adhesions that have sprouted in my chest from my other ports. It takes him nearly two hours to wrangle it from my chest, and when Mum tells me after I wake up, I can't help but think it was the last piece of my old life fighting to stay within me.

'He wasn't happy,' says Mum.

I'm just grateful I was sedated. Being in a medically induced coma forces the body – and the brain – into a state of rest.

When the pathology on my port comes back, the results indicate that it had been culturing some nasty bacteria and that it was clotted. In the final days before my transplant, I had spiked fevers and got my first and last UTI. I had suspected my port was infected, but because I was about to die, it seemed nonsensical to bring this to anyone's attention. In the days after I'm extubated (taken off life support), I think how lucky I am that the surgery went ahead. These days, there would be no chance of transplant surgery going ahead if you were on the edge of septicaemia.

My seventh – and final port – is the size of a one-dollar coin and is inserted on the inside of my left arm under local anaesthetic. I'd always been deep in the arms of propofol when I had a port insertion, and I would later wish I'd been asleep for this one.

Tom, the head of the radiology department – a brilliant, kind man I am also friends with on 'the outside' – has trouble from the beginning. I keep telling him, 'It's me. I'm sorry, it's just my veins.'

Julie, the CF liaison nurse assisting Tom, is eyeing off my striped pyjama pants while valiantly trying to distract me from what is happening on the other side of my body.

'I love your pants. I want your pants.'

'They wouldn't fit you, Julie,' says Tom.

'Tom!' says Julie. 'Carly – your thoughts, please?'

'I refuse to say anything on account that Tom has a scalpel in his hand.'

'I thought you'd defend my honour!'

'Not this time!'

Tom makes a small incision on the inside of my arm, and for the next two hours his fingers wriggle around inside. If you can imagine lifting the skin of a chicken to shove in a bouquet garni, this is as close to the experience as I can take you. I feel every cut, stitch, push and pull to get the line in place.

Two weeks later, I present at emergency. My upper arm is an angry shade of red, the port site throbbing and swollen. It's clear something disastrous is unfolding. An ultrasound finds an eight-inch blood clot wrapped around the catheter of the port. There are jitters through radiology and the transplant team because clots are unstable and can split off and travel to your lungs or brain, which means a pulmonary embolism or a catastrophic stroke. I imagine this clot as a boa constrictor wrapped around the catheter in my artery, its form heaving with a pulse of its own, my blood treacle thick. Through various scans, it's ascertained the clot is unstable, so the transplant team are loath to remove the port. My basilic vein has snapped shut like a Venus flytrap and a map of veins flushes up my arm, across my neck and chest like a series of tributaries that can still be seen today.

A couple of years later, I get an infection that warrants a course of IV vancomycin – the last line of defence against the superbug MRSA. Not long after this, the port stops working altogether. Mercifully, it's removed without any trouble, and I'm put on warfarin, an anti-coagulant whose natural derivative is used for rat poison. To add insult to injury, I'm told I'm now 'clotty', which precludes me from ever having another port because of this new propensity to congeal.

Eros et Thanatos. Sex and death. Whether we like it or not, they are inextricably linked, and for me, sex helped save my life. While I was on the transplant list, the only physical activity I was interested in was that of a sexual nature. When my sister left for London, she wrote in a card: *Have plenty of sex and keep those lungs working!* And so, I dutifully obliged.

Ollie and I got together on the night of my twenty-first birthday. I'd wanted to celebrate this milestone because I was convinced it would be the last party I'd ever have; the next time these people saw each other would be at my funeral.

A few weeks earlier I had met Ollie at dinner with my crew of friends. Although we'd run in the same circles for years and been to countless parties together, we had never met. He was an unassuming character, and after hearing stories about him drinking to the point of passing out in churchyards, I was not impressed. What I didn't realise at the time was that I was just as much of a pisshead as he was – the only difference being that I always managed to get myself home.

Ollie was one of three boys who turned up to my twenty-first in a suit. The day before, I'd made a mental list of who I wanted to kiss at midnight. Ollie wasn't on it, but I was taken with his cheeky grin and laconic drawl as we lay under paper lanterns on the lawn, talking and laughing. At around 9.30 pm, much to my surprise, an explosion of fireworks had lit up the sky over our house, the river below glowing with starbursts of colour. It turned out that Dad had organised the pyrotechnic crew who were responsible for lighting up Brisbane city at midnight to ring in the new year. At first, I didn't know what was happening, but when my sister screamed at me, 'They're for you!' I was delighted. People would later tell me the light show could be seen all the way from Mount Coot-tha. The other thing I didn't know was that the pyrotechnic crew had left some of the leftover fireworks for my dad and our next-door neighbour to detonate at midnight. Dad and Noel had a history of lighting expired flares at midnight and casting them over the water, and tonight was no different. As the new year approached, they once again set some mangroves on fire across the river. As the clock struck twelve, and T-Shirt's 'You Sexy Thing' punctured the humid Brisbane air, I pulled Ollie in for a kiss.

While Dad and Noel were busy nearly blowing themselves up, I was busy kissing Ollie. We drank and kissed the night away, then watched the blush of the new year's first sunrise together. It was 1998.

It turned out that I was Ollie's first girlfriend. A fortnight after my twenty-first, we were in the biggest of sex fogs. It was the best sex I'd ever had, and we were libertine to the bone – sex in public, sex in the pool, sex in the ocean, sex in hospital, sex on the kitchen bench, sex on industrial waste bins in city alleyways. Sex everywhere. Hanging out naked with other people. It was all very hedonistic.

But reality came knocking soon enough. In April, four months after I was put on the transplant list, I learnt that my friend Jamie was dying. He was eighteen. Jamie hadn't been sick enough to go on the transplant list. In fact, he'd been relatively lucky with his lungs – it was his gut that gave him the most grief. He was thin as a beanpole because of his malabsorption issues; no matter how much he ate or how many times a day he was tube fed, he just couldn't put on weight. He loved nothing more than driving in his beloved Holden ute and would often ask if I wanted anything while he was out. Jamie would bring me back treats whether I had asked for them or not, and one night he presented me with my favourite – a Violet Crumble. In that moment I could not love him more.

'So, I went to get a kebab and I park in a loading zone. Two cops come up to me and say, "You're parked in a loading zone." I say, "I know – I'm loading up on a kebab."'

The police couldn't contain their laughter, so they let him go. Only Jamie could have gotten away with something like that.

By July, Jamie had a chest infection that cascaded into double pneumonia. I was also an inpatient at the time and Ollie was about to pick me up from the hospital to take me out for the day. Before I left, I walked into Jamie's room – a single room, the dying room – and he said, 'The doctor says I'm gonna die.'

I took his hand and nodded. 'I know, mate.'

'I'm going home.'

'That's good.'

'I'm scared.'

'That's okay, too,' I said. 'But you'll have Bec looking after you. You couldn't have anyone better.' Bec was our favourite nurse. His face relaxed a little.

I held it together as we said goodbye, but when I walked out of the dying room I needed to pause in the hallway and compose myself. We were on the freeway driving into the city, when I said to Ollie, 'Jamie's going home.'

Ollie was silent.

'Do you know what that means? He's going to die.'

Nothing.

Ollie turned the music up and exited the expressway. I leant into the passenger door and cried. At the time it felt like the gravity of losing my friend didn't mean anything to Ollie. It wasn't until years later that I realised Ollie would have been terrified. At the time I thought he was being insensitive, but hearing about Jamie's fate would have reminded Ollie that my own death was imminent.

⚘

When I was on the transplant list, I was losing a kilo every week because my body was churning through the calories just trying to breathe, and so the idea of artificial feeding was thrown into the mix. I shut the idea down immediately and doubled down when asked if I'd like to try a nasogastric (NG) tube. Since I was a kid, whenever I attempted to thread an NG tube up my nose and into my stomach, it would pierce the cartilage inside my nose and I would bleed. I already knew I was going to die, so what was the point in having a feeding tube that would only extend my suffering? If my doctors were serious about feeding, they would have had me on a total parenteral nutrition (TPN) infusion through my port, but instead of this less intrusive method, here they were espousing the virtues of a 'button' or a 'peg'.

I asked them how they planned to surgically place the tube because, at this point, a general anaesthetic would have probably killed me. They could have given me 'twilight sedation', but this would have been ineffective due to my high tolerance for opioids, barbiturates and anaesthetics. Having a surgeon cutting their way into my stomach while I was conscious didn't appeal to me. I didn't want a feeding tube poking out of my stomach; I had enough scars. The top of my body was already a constellation of markings, and my stomach was the last bastion; I was determined it would remain untouched. The only scar I wanted on my body would be when the surgeons cut me in half for transplant. My doctors didn't argue the point. And so, when I died, it would be with a perfect porcelain stomach, untouched by the flick of a surgeon's scalpel. At some point, you need to stop. Enough with the heroics.

But I wasn't ready to die quite yet. Instead of hospital meals, I subsisted on a steady supply of fairy floss, puréed apples, passionfruit-flavoured yoghurt and garlic prawns from my local fish-and-chippery. When a body reaches a palliative level of illness, it doesn't need fuel. When I did eat, I would have violent bouts of coughing that would sometimes lead to syncope. People talk about pooping unicorns – I was busy throwing up rainbows.

One day, I was sitting in my doctor's office as we lamented the absence of my appetite. Digging his spine into his ergonomic chair, he interlaced his fingers behind his head and thrust his chest forward, as though this was going to lend him a thicker membrane of wisdom. His floppy dark-blond hair brushed each side of his head like a curtain as he handed me a tissue so I could remove my scarlet-coloured lipstick.

'How blue are you today?' he asked.

I wiped off my lipstick.

'Your colour isn't great So, it's a definite no for the peg?'

'Yes. No. It's a "no" for another blemish on my body.'

'We're going to have to get you to eat somehow.'

'How?'

'There are other ways,' he said, raising his brows.

'Such as?'

He leant forward. 'Have you got a dealer?'

'A what?'

'You know ...'

'Oh, you mean like "herbal remedy?"' I replied, pointing quotation marks into the stale air.

'Um, yes.'

'Do you?'

'Um, no. I mean, absolutely not.'

He reasoned that if I could tolerate marijuana, we could kill two birds with one stone – alleviate my physical pain and give me the munchies so I could gain enough weight to stabilise, making me stronger for transplant.

Ollie and I were living an experimental lifestyle – it was the nineties, and we had no shortage of friends shooting heroin and all sorts of gear – so it was easy to source something as banal as pot.

I couldn't smoke it, so we were going to have to bake it into something, but by the time we picked it up, we were already on route to the beach to have a KFC picnic. Ollie rolled a joint, and we took turns inhaling. One tentative puff had me coughing myself into a disconcerting shade of lavender. I persevered. I got stoned. I called Mum.

'Well? Did it make you hungry?' she asked.

'If there was a cow standing in front of me, I'd just start carving it up.'

'Carls, this could be what we need to get you to transplant!'

Ollie and I drove to McDonald's, then we stopped at a lolly shop where I scraped half a kilo of diabetes into a brown paper bag, before driving back to Ollie's where I ate like a starving refugee on his bed. The tang of the sauce on my burger, the grease from the chicken nuggets, and the sickly-sweet flavour of lemonade on my tongue was thrilling because at that point I never thought I would feel hungry again. When I began to cough, Ollie instinctively picked me up and carried me to the shower where I expectorated the entire contents of my stomach. All the calories, fat and sustenance – gone.

The next day, I woke up feeling like my head was floating outside my body. Ollie and I had an argument, and I left his house in a blazing fit of rage. I was sitting in a gutter when I thought the most sensible thing to do would be to stand up and walk in front of the bus that was flying up the hill. The irony about trying to throw myself in front of a bus was that by the time the thought had connected to my body, I was too breathless to even walk onto the road.

'Fuck,' I thought. 'I'm even shit at trying to kill myself.'

I spent the next couple of hours thinking that if I couldn't die by my own hand, then I had no other option but to live.

Knowing that I needed help, I fell into the care of the psychiatrist who had done my initial assessment for my transplant work-up. I had been on antidepressants since I was nineteen, but the weight of what was happening in my life was fast becoming a burden far too heavy for me to shoulder alone. Friends were dying and I felt guilty for being alive, even though I was so close to death myself. I was prescribed another type of antidepressant; each week I would return to the hospital's grim psychiatric unit.

Foolishly or optimistically, I gave pot another try and had my second round of psychosis.

I reported back to my doctor that our idea had not gone well.

'I'm sorry to hear it,' he said.

'So am I.'

I had nearly killed myself just trying to eat.

Several weeks later, I was sitting on the floor of our rental sorting through my music library. I had to sit on a cushion because my arse was so bony it would bruise like a piece of manhandled fruit. Being shackled to oxygen 24/7, I tried to do as much as I could without coughing myself into a state of semi-consciousness.

As I unfurled my legs and grabbed the corner of the couch to hoist my bag of bones off the floor, I felt compelled to look at what I had become. Not who, but what. In the bathroom mirror stood the husk of a girl. What had been dark circles beneath my eyes were now purple half-moons. My cheeks were hollow, my lips blue and my nose dry from the constant flow of supplemental oxygen. What I found most disconcerting was I had a look I had only seen on the faces of my friends just before they died, a look that was reserved for the dying – a fusion of fear, disbelief and wonder. I could see death a few paces in front, eager to trip me up. Where some people glared at death, hurtling towards it unafraid, others would panic, unsure whether to acknowledge it or not. I stared blankly, stunned that this was me. The woman in the mirror was me.

I gathered my oxygen tubing, shuffled out of the bathroom and into my bedroom where I stripped off. It was a curious sight. I knew I'd lost a lot of weight but still I recoiled at the cavernous gap between my thighs. As my eyes moved up and down my body, I saw hipbones poking out like little keels trying to escape my skin, paper-thin and translucent after months of being under fluorescent lights in my hospital room. I could see my clavicles for the first time, and I rapped at them with my knuckles as if to say hello. My breasts resembled mosquito bites, and just above them, a needle dangled out of my chest. I no longer felt like a sexual being; I was both repulsed and mesmerised by what I saw. I thought I'd enjoy being thin, but it was painful. Everything hurt. Looking at photographs now, I see that I was strangely beautiful. My face was fine-featured like Mia Farrow's, with cheekbones that reached to the sky, and wide, searching green eyes.

Ollie still thought I was beautiful, and he would cushion my body on his. Strangely enough, sex proved to be an unlikely lifesaver. Long gone were the days when I stumbled through the doors of emergency glammed up and wearing stilettos, slurring to the nurses at triage that I was a doctor 'on call'.

'See? I have a beeper and everything,' I'd say, pointing to the little black box on my hip.

My CF friend Matt always kept me updated with the code for the doors, so it was easy getting in and out. I would pass out in my bed wearing my stilettos and have a jab of morphine for my incoming hangover.

'I'm *dying*,' I would say to Ollie. 'The least you can do is service me and help me breathe.'

THE PAIN I HAVE AFTER my transplant surgery is unusual. Even with an epidural and injections of morphine, I am still in agony. In the 1990s, doctors are frugal with pain relief, and there is never a time I'm pain free. It's like nothing I've ever felt before, and I'm genuinely afraid that the pain might kill me. While I feel immense gratitude, I am physically, mentally and existentially crushed. You cannot and do not heal in an environment that has cradled you in your sickness.

The day I have my epidural removed, I'm relocated to the less acute ICU. My friends Tammy and Andrew have arrived to see me, but I barely feel the tight embrace of Tammy's arms because I've never felt pain on this scale. A couple of years later, I write: *I like to think I would have waited until my parents and friends had left the room before I cocked a gun to my head and squeezed the trigger, so fierce was the pain when the epidural was ripped.* It's the kind of pain where you pray for a mercy bullet. I think – and hope – my clamshell cut will burst open and spray chunks of lung and bone and wire all over the walls, splattering the faces of the nursing staff and surrounding patients in beautiful, sweeping shades of vermilion. I'd have an open chest, but the relief would be immense because I would be dead. I am honest about this: if I'd had a firearm, I would have used it. It would have been an easy choice. The pain was so immense that someone could have taken a butter knife to my chest and I wouldn't have felt so much as a scratch.

Yet, for such a serious place, and possibly because of it, much hilarity ensues in ICU. One day my high school friend Georgie visits and I'm sitting up in bed. She's just one of several people I flash my boobs to. In the weeks to come, I happily raise my gown to show anyone who wants to see my breast lift, and even for the people who don't. I flash the staff from the Mater, including my doctor, Peter, who is one of my current transplant consultants. But back to Georgie.

'Look at my breast lift – thank you, Medicare!'

Georgie turns a curious shade of green and Mum ferries her out of the room. When I still have a catheter in, I say to my friends mid-conversation, 'I'm peeing *right now.*' There's a night when a lovely male nurse hears my whole life story. I can't stop talking simply because I have the breath to do it. Granted, at this point I still have an epidural and my pain is under control. Mum writes in The Transplant Diaries: *Carly has verbal diarrhoea.*

In the first week after my transplant, I manage to impress people by simply lying awake in bed. When I fart for the first time, the nurses cheer. The first time I sit in a chair is cause célèbre. My first walk is like a tickertape parade, but I don't hear it because I am certain I'm going to die. The news of my first shit – brutal in its delivery – sweeps across the intensive care unit, garnering nods of approval, wishes of 'well done' and fist-pumping, as though I've just won an Olympic medal for Queen and country.

While seeing, tasting, smelling and hearing myself die is the strangest thing I've ever done, recovering from death ushers in a whole other level of feeling. I physically ache to be who I was before: Carly – the fierce, riotous, wildly self-assured, take-no-prisoners firebrand. But how does one bridge the gap between dying and living? We have become so familiar with closing the aperture on life, doing the opposite seems like an unnatural progression. When you are dying, you die. Dying doesn't offer any junctures. I'd defied the natural order of things. I had prepared myself for death but instead of bursting back into my renewed life I want to scarper into the wilderness like a mortally wounded animal. It feels like the world is pushing its way into my body without my permission, and that any evidence of my old life has disappeared.

And here's the rub: I have come back too fast. Like a spaceship breaking up on re-entry, I've come from a place of peace only to return to life with an unnatural sense of violence. It is too much, and I break apart; my mind splinters off into the atmosphere. I had not expected this; my return to life is brutal.

In ICU, nights are hell. In the first week after my transplant, I have two that are almost impossible to bear. Not long after I am extubated a nurse who is everything a nurse shouldn't be – cruel, dismissive and cavalier – is on duty.

It's been drilled into me that I need to tell someone every time I feel something different, so when I tell her I have chest pain, she rolls her eyes.

'You're fine.'

I know that I am not fine. It feels like a pneumothorax, which is when air leaks into the space between your lungs and your chest wall. Hours later – at my insistence – she calls radiology in a huff, and they bring in a portable X-ray machine. It turns out I have a collapsed lung, which leads me to think I'm going to die again. Adding to the anguish, she fails to tell me that Dad had been fifty metres away in the waiting room the whole time. It doesn't take long for my terror to turn to anger. It only comes down to dumb luck that my lung re-inflates on its own without the need for another chest tube.

Eight days post-surgery, I have the final two drains pulled out of my chest. Chest tubes drain the excess blood and pus from the lungs. The four that have been sewn into my chest are nearly as thick as garden hoses. While the removal of the first three isn't pleasant, it's a fairly seamless process. The removal of the last drain is excruciating when the nurse rips it out while it's still stitched into my skin. I gasp with the pain; I see stars. Never before have I seen stars.

'Oh, didn't see those there,' she says nonchalantly, and snips the last few sutures out of my skin.

With the drains gone, I am left with four gaping wounds. At first I leak, but the leaking turns into a spillway – forming a syrupy pool in my lap. It doesn't matter how many pads of gauze I pack on; any exertion has pus spraying all over me – the force behind it much like ejaculation.

One day, when my sister, Nikki, and our friend Gina are visiting, I'm crying and I blurt out, 'I'm jizzing pus.'

'What?' they ask.

'I'M JIZZING PUS.'

Instead of sympathy, they howl with laughter. I roll my eyes, push gauze hard into my trunk and, seeing as I have my appetite back, reach for more food to shovel into my mouth.

There are many impossible nights, but existentially, the worst night comes after I've been moved to ICU 3. I might be on morphine, but with the pissy doses I'm being given, I'm impeccably lucid.

It's late, maybe around midnight. I'm lying semi-upright in bed, trying to pretzel my body into some sort of comfortable position, when I overhear the dangling threads of a conversation nearby. I'm in a pod at the entrance of the unit, which means I'm next to the family waiting room where inconceivable discussions take place. The door is open, and I find myself privy to a decision a family is having to make.

I can't work out exactly what the exchange is about, but it soon becomes clear through the guttural moans that they're contemplating whether to withdraw their daughter's life support and donate her organs.

'But she's still moving,' says a family member.

I knew this to be a Lazarus movement. When a neural pathway passes through the spinal column but not through the brain, brain-dead patients can still make movements while functioning on life support. This reflex can be preceded by slight shivering motions of the patient's arms or goosebumps on the arms and torso. The patient's arms can flex at the elbows then lift towards the neck or chin before touching or crossing over, much like a prayer position. Short exhalations have also been observed, even after life support has been withdrawn. It is not the harbinger of a miraculous event, despite the family desperately wanting it to be so. It is the zenith of cruelty.

'But her heart's still beating – I can see it on the monitor.'

'That's the ventilator keeping her heart and lungs functioning. When we remove the life support system, her heart and lungs will stop working,' says the doctor.

'I don't understand. Why can't you do anything?' asks a man.

They discuss the catastrophic injury to her brain.

'But we could bring her home?'

'I'm so sorry, but that wouldn't be possible. The machines can't be taken home.'

'But what if we could? I've seen it on TV where people bring their kids home on life support.'

'Those people are still alive.'

'She *is* alive.'

'I'm so sorry, but her brain has been damaged to such a point that everything she needs to keep her organs functioning relies solely on the ventilator.'

The crying. I imagine rivers of tears flooding the corridors, and people with mops and buckets.

'Have you ever discussed organ donation with your daughter?'

They had.

'Would you ever consider donating your daughter's organs?'

They would.

'But she's still alive,' says her mother.

'No, she's not. She's gone, love,' says the father gently.

Then another male voice: 'So now you just want her for her organs?'

'That's not the case at all. This is something we bring up when an injury like this occurs in such a young and otherwise healthy person. It's ultimately your decision and we don't have to discuss it any further if you don't want to.'

'So, what happens if we do donate?' asks her mum.

'There are some other tests that need to be done to ensure that brain death has occurred.'

'But you said that it has.'

'Yes, I did. But there are legal protocols we need to follow. Would you like to speak to one of our transplant coordinators? They'll be able to answer any questions you have.'

'So, we don't get to see you turn her life support off? We won't be there when she dies?'

'I'm afraid not. Because we need to take her to theatre to perform the transplant surgery, she will pass away in theatre.'

The mother speaks. 'Everything,' she says. 'You can have everything.'

There's a lowering of conversation, and that's when I know that the doctor has left to get the transplant coordinator and the relevant paperwork organised. The process takes hours. There's another gathering in the waiting room where doctors field more questions about how the transplant surgery will unfold. They explain that the body is treated with the utmost dignity and sensitivity; that the surgery is performed just as other surgeries are – with care and kind, gentle hands.

'So, you don't just cut her up and take out what you want and leave her to die?'

'Not at all. If anything,' explains the doctor, 'we take even more care because we know what a gift this is.'

Though I can't hear it, it is like the room is breathing again; like the walls have let go a collective sigh.

There's a part of me that wants to bang on the wall and tell them that what they're doing is the most incredible and noble thing anyone could ever do, that their decision is going to save lives. But I know I've been privy to an exchange so intimate and rare, its breadth is impossible to comprehend.

FROM THE DAY I HAVE my transplant to the day I leave hospital three weeks later, not a day goes by when there isn't a crisis of some kind.

My sister writes in The Transplant Diaries on Monday 24 August:

> *Carly's upset because she still has the tube in. She thought something was wrong. She asked if she was alive, then she asked what was happening with the house. Then she asked to see Dad. They've completely switched off the ventilator, so she's breathing by herself. We showed Carly the graph so she knew how she should be breathing. She's getting REALLY agitated and wants the tube out NOW.*
>
> *She's coherent as to what's going on. She's poking faces – not frowning anymore! Her strength has really improved in her hands, she's really starting to show her true colours – thumping the bed because she wants the tube out. All conversation was with the alphabet board.*

My doctors are confounded by how much sedation I need to be put back into an induced coma. My levels of sedation are unusually high: around twenty-five times the amount required to sedate a person of my age and size. When I see photos of myself in a dreamless sleep, tentacles of tubes spilling from my body, I look like I'm in a state of perfect peace, strangely beautiful because I am untethered from this world and in a place I cannot name.

Once I'm out of ICU and back on the respiratory ward, I'm sharing a four-bed room with three elderly women. As I'd discovered at the Mater, old people snore. Pre-transplant, I'd often slept in the TV room because it was the only place where there was relative silence. About ten days post-transplant, I begin to unravel. Not an hour goes by where I'm not having a panic attack, and the exhaustion on every level is taking its toll. I've only had fleeting grabs of sleep in ICU, and rest is crucial to recovering from one of the biggest surgeries a human can have. By the time I'm moved into the only single room on the ward, I'm deep within the arms of delirium. I intermittently laugh and cry as goblins materialise out of the walls and fly around the room. I'm happy because I've always wanted to see a goblin, but it's strange because I always imagined they would move at great speed, whereas these ones seem to be flying in slow motion. By the time the goblins disappear, all I care about is coming into the quiet of my own heart, but this will take some time. Mum asks the psychiatrist to see me because I'm depressed and can't stop crying. We realise that I have gone without my antidepressants for ten days, which has put me into a state of withdrawal, so I begin taking them again that afternoon.

When I'm finally allowed day leave, I am told in no uncertain terms that I need to rest. We were meant to move into our new house when I was abruptly called up for surgery. Since then, Mum's bestie, Marion, moved us in, and I'm so excited about seeing it that I need a bolus of morphine when I get back to the hospital that afternoon. I'm ready to return to life and think rest is for the weak, telling myself that I've done enough resting for several lifetimes.

Because I don't fancy the insipid showers at the hospital, if I'm on a home visit, I shower in my parents' new bathroom, which has glass panels on the roof so you can see the sky. It's my first taste of independence, showering on my own. I can't have a bath yet because my incision can't be wet for long, so I take my time and I manage to walk up a flight of stairs, feeling victorious as I reach the parapet. When I look down to see my family's reaction, they've missed it.

'Um, hello? I just bounded up the stairs!'

My parents, Nikki and Ollie think it's hilarious that they've missed this milestone.

'Still a bit breathless,' I say.

'Maybe you got an asthmatic's lungs?' Mum quips.

'Yeah, maybe,' I wheeze.

While it seems trivial, the breathlessness that day is the first sign my body is rejecting my donor lungs. After an organ is transplanted into a body, patients take powerful immunosuppressants for the rest of their lives so the body doesn't 'reject' the organ. I bring this up with the head of the heart transplant unit, and while he dismisses my concerns, I have a niggling feeling that things are about to go south.

By the time Monday rolls around, I am dying. Again.

31 August 1998

Rang at 7.00 am. Carly had a bad night. At 9.00 pm she couldn't stop coughing. She slept well but the hospital rang me at 10.00 pm to say she is having a bronchoscopy and biopsy. They didn't say she was rejecting, but when I got there, she was on oxygen and had a terrible headache. She thought she had asthma, but it was rejection.

It's 11.45 am – the anaesthetist is trying to find a vein.

Ross is here too, and Carly is wearing a white rose in memory of Princess Diana. She is in extreme pain, like someone is sitting on her chest. She is having morphine and Endone.

12.30 pm – we are now waiting in the procedure room. They couldn't find a vein, so they may have to put in a central line. Carly was taken down by wheelchair with oxygen like before her transplant. She is so upset but when she tried to cry, she couldn't because it hurt too much.

12.50 pm – Scott just arrived to do the bronchoscopy. He is concerned as she has no veins, and they may have to call in another anaesthetist. He tried to make us feel reassured that this can happen. Some don't get any rejection, but you can go through this at any time. Scott had been sick over the weekend, but Doctor Hazel had been in touch to monitor her. They knew about the breathlessness.

1.05 pm – Scott just came out of theatre to tell me he got a vein and that he is going down to bronc her now.

1.20 pm – Carly is now in the recovery room for about an hour. Scott said he could tell by X-rays today that she is rejecting, and he'll know the results of the biopsy in a couple of hours. He sucked out her right upper lung. They have started a prednisone drip, but the cannula looks like it will pack in any minute. Ollie is here now.

5.15 pm – Scott and team just came down and said, 'You have rejection' but the results haven't come back from the lab yet. They have given her a bolus of steroids – 500 mg and 750 mg IV once daily for a couple of days. Carly seems a lot better tonight than this morning and will now have a shower with my help.

When the biopsy results come in, we're told that the rejection is 'significant'. As Mum writes: *Whatever that means. Is that more than yesterday's 'reasonable'?* Scott had called Melbourne and London, trying to work out the best course of action. In the end I'm given potent doses of intravenous methylprednisolone. A quarter of a century later, not much has changed in the way of treating rejection.

As for my anti-rejection medication, I'm on a triumvirate of immunosuppressants I will take for the rest of my life, but the levels of my anti-rejection meds are far higher than they should be, giving me dreadful headaches. By this stage, doctors are using the tiniest veins in my thumbs and feet, and were I not in such agony, I would have pleaded for a central line. My arms and hands are varying shades of violet and yellow, and my hospital room looks like a florist with flowers arriving nearly daily.

On day twelve, I write in The Transplant Diaries:

> *In the end, I manage to convince them to let me go home, but only if I rest adequately, due to the trouble I found myself in after yesterday's efforts ... I was so happy to be escaping the ward and walking in the winter sunshine. The day was so beautiful. Warm and crystalline blue – as if the weather has cleared like my lungs have. We arrived home, had some lunch, and I hit the couch and cranked up some Nick Cave and set about writing this. Mid-shower, Ollie arrived, so he helped me in that respect (ha) with drying off, as did Mum. I had all hands on deck, so to speak. Ollie and I had our first bed cuddle since the transplant, and that alone was worth making it through the surgery. It was time to leave, so Ollie and I drove off into the sunset chanting 'She Caught the Katy' from* The Blues Brothers.

That night, clumps of hair from the back of my head come away in my hands. Literal handfuls of hair. I write: *Is nothing sacred?* And then: *I am going to have to be the strongest, most tenacious I have ever been. The bravest I have ever been is not going to be enough this time.*

These words have nothing to do with losing my hair and everything to do with my survival.

I have another bronchoscopy on day thirteen and am given a slower-acting form of morphine. I throw up and am given massive quantities of intravenous pain relief and general anaesthesia to get me to sleep. In The Transplant Diaries, Mum writes: *Scott's words are: 'She's a hard one to keep asleep – she just keeps talking. She's giving me grey hair.'*

Following the bronchoscopy, Scott talks to my parents. While he thinks my lungs look good, my X-ray doesn't reflect this. He's worried the rejection is ramping up. But X-rays can be deceiving as the lymphatic glands are cut during transplant and don't often repair themselves. Fluid has to drain somewhere, and sometimes it can collect in the pleura of the lung, which can present its own dangers. Scott also wants to start treatment for cytomegalovirus (CMV), which necessitates a central line so that I can do the infusions myself once I get home. But first, another bronchoscopy. Scott is far from happy with my X-ray and has slept on whether to do a bronc or not but when he hears me cough, he says, 'That's just made up my mind. I'm doing it now.'

When the results come back, Scott tells us the bad news: the rejection is still raging, so I need more megadoses of steroids. That night, I'm taken back to ICU so that a central line can be inserted into my chest for infusions of steroids and the powerful anti-viral ganciclovir. A changeover to a new anti-rejection drug is mentioned, but I'm in too much pain for this news to register. Being back in ICU is terrifying, and I worry about leaving in a body bag. My pain levels are unmanageable with the meagre doses of morphine I'm on. First, I'm given 2.5 mg, then another 2.5 mg, and finally they give me a 10 mg bolus, as well as having my slower acting morphine increased.

I miss Laura's twenty-first birthday party. Laura has been by my side through it all. I will go on to miss four out of five of my closest friends' parties, which is devastating to me at the time. Ollie leaves me a note that night: *Hello baby, wish you could be with me tonight – we'll make up for your lack of partying later. You'll never miss another party after this. See you tomorrow, beautiful.*

On the first full moon in my new body, the pain settles. I go home for the afternoon, stand under the shower with the glass panels where I can see the sky, and nearly fall over backwards trying to find the full moon.

While I'm still in hospital, Mum takes me to get my licence renewed before I get moon face from the steroids. Steroids have an abundance of nasty side effects like violent mood swings and insomnia, but when I get upset Mum knows it is just the frustration of one step forward and three steps back. It's as if any strength I have is being pushed through a sieve.

After several doses of mega-roids, I look five months pregnant. I've put on seven kilograms of fluid overnight and feel like an overloaded zeppelin. One night when Ollie visits, he walks out of the room because I am unrecognisable. Peeing out seven kilograms of fluid in one night is physically taxing. Exactly a fortnight post-transplant I have two blood transfusions after which I begin throwing up. Scott is concerned, but because my X-ray looks okay and my chest doesn't sound too crackly, he's happy to hold off on another bronchoscopy. He tells us that night that I have three things on my side – great family support, good nutrition, and a brilliant set of donor lungs. In his words, 'the best set we have ever seen'. I have my first decent sleep since the surgery. The steroids work, and I begin taking a newer anti-rejection medication called tacrolimus. I might look like a chipmunk from the steroids, but according to Mum, I've had enough and am 'over it'. I just want to get better.

⚘

10 September 1998

She doesn't like being left alone and cries when I leave.

These eleven words sum up my post-transplant experience in hospital. It's not that I don't enjoy my own company, but any sense of safety vanishes when Mum leaves. I never feel safe when I'm by myself. Whenever life gets quiet, a low hum of menace pervades. I feel guilty crying in front of Mum, so I hold off until she's left for the day. People talk about their 'ride or dies'. Mum is so much more than that. She's my oxygen mask.

Then, one night on the way home, Mum hits a dog with her car, goes into shock and loses part of her short-term memory. I realise it's not just the dog. It's a culmination of everything: the last day, the last week, the last month, the last year, the last twenty-one years.

One thing she's never forgotten was when I was sitting up in a chair in ICU, talking to her with my oxygen mask on.

'So ... I saw Nana.'

'What do you mean?'

'Well, I walked into this tunnel, and there she was, and I was so happy to see her.'

I tell Mum that instead of being pleased to see me, my grandmother was standing in a cliché of light, telling me very sternly to go back to where I had come from.

'It's not your time. You're not ready,' she said.

I walk towards her.

'But Nana …'

'Turn the fuck around and go back.'

Mum looks at me.

'It's not like Nana to swear,' I say.

'What do you think that was about?' Mum asks.

'I think I died on the table.'

'I had the same thought.'

There is a diary entry where Mum writes: *I am really tired. It has started to rain, and I feel like I could curl up and have a sleep myself.*

Every time I read this over the ensuing years, I feel like I've been gutted like a fish.

WHEN I WAS FIRST TAKEN off life support, I noticed that my voice was squeaky. I sounded like a chipmunk, and we deduced this was from the tube being down my throat. But months later, my voice isn't any better. I see an ENT specialist who puts a scope down my throat and declares that my left vocal cord is paralysed.

'Will it get better?' I ask.

'You could try speech therapy, but it may be permanent.'

'How often does this happen post-surgery?'

'About one in one hundred thousand cases.'

It is never explained how this happened – only that it has.

My stomach lurches, but there's a spark of optimism. Speech therapy could work, and I'll be able to sing again. Mum takes me to see a speech therapist for a few months, but I walk away feeling more defeated with each visit. There is no improvement. I can't sing like I used to, and I will never sing like I used to. I can't even scream. Where I could once command a room – or a hall, an oval or a campsite – with my booming voice, my essence has been reduced. Was I ever more than my voice?

My voice was a gift. A weapon. My currency. My voice was how I steered myself in the world and was often my greatest ally. It was always with me. It didn't matter where I was – I could, and did, use it. I could create incredible sounds. I had twenty-one years with this voice, but when I woke up after my transplant, it lay paralysed across my larynx in a state of eternal dysphonia.

I miss the voice I was born with. In a medical paper I read: *Vocal cord paralysis following endotracheal intubation is a rare complication with an incidence of less than 0.1%.* While my fractured voice may be a metaphor for life, I've buttressed myself against the world and still sing every day. Some days I squeak like a prepubescent boy, and some days I sound like Aretha Franklin. In a deliberate act of radical acceptance, I've had to learn to embrace the mystery, because singing with one vocal cord can be tricky.

I used to think that there was a redundant, unlovable, unusable piece of me that would be strung across my throat forever, like a bell that won't peal when it's rung. I now find comfort that there's a fleshy piece of the old me that sits there dead, making me brittle of voice. Often, when I speak (or squeak), I have to think about how I'm going to hold my head, so the sound comes out cleanly because my pitch, tone and projection are the opposite of what my voice once was.

Was losing my voice a blessing? No. And yet, it's been a powerful lesson in economy and expansion. Economy of words, sound, emotion, and so many other things. Expansion in empathy for myself. Just as music had sustained me before my surgery, it fortifies me afterwards. When you're born with an incurable disease, you learn to fit around it, and if you're lucky, sometimes your disease fits around you. Living systems adapt by transforming themselves and as such, I became a mistress of adaptation.

Growing up, I always had high expectations of myself. From as far back as I can remember I wanted to be an actress or a singer. I had also wanted to be a park ranger, a librarian and a post mistress. When it was explained to me that I'd have to clean public toilets, the park ranger dream was over, but I still tended to my rainforest most days, keeping a journal where I would write about each plant. I drew up plans for a fishpond, joined the Koala Foundation, subscribed to an environmental magazine with trailblazing topics such as biodiversity, and covered my 'Environmental' concertina file with animal rights and Save The Trees stickers. When I was around eleven, I tried to save a forest. Not a big one, but an important little ecosystem all the same. The bucolic piece of land was in my street and was being sold so a house could be built, which meant that a whole lot of trees were going to be – in my mind – murdered. Me and a local icon called Heritage got together and put out the call, and our movement became such a sensation that the children's afternoon TV program *Wombat* filmed a report on our fight to save the trees. While we lost our bid to preserve that piece of land, it was an experience being on television and confirmed I wanted to be an actress, preferably one who had a PhD in English literature.

Being on stage, for me, was a spiritual experience – otherworldly. It was every perfect moment coalesced into one where I was braided with the character I was playing. There is an electricity. Your body pings with invisible sparks. You hear and feel the hum of your blood. It thumps with urgency in your ears, everything is alive and as soon as you exit the stage, you want to do it all over again. And you're so high that you would do it again naked.

After finishing year twelve I auditioned for drama school by performing a raging monologue from August Strindberg's *Miss Julie*. After a second audition of this searing and nuanced piece I am accepted into the program.

Following my audition, I sat down with one of the heads of the drama department.

'We'd love to take you into the acting strand,' he said.

At drama school in 1995, the acting strand had an intake of around twelve students, while the open strand accepted well over one hundred. I was thrilled to be chosen for the acting strand, but my heart dropped because I knew I would have to decline. My disease was progressing; the acting strand is voice and movement oriented, and the physicality it demanded in such a small collective of students meant that I would have needed to *not* be sick. I didn't want to let anyone down, so I politely declined. I left the room feeling as though the eye of luck had opened, but once it took a look at me it snapped shut. Did I ever look at that elite group of actors and think, *that could have been me*? Of course I did. But instead of dwelling on it, I focused on what I could do, rather than what I couldn't.

In 1996, my doctor Simon advised me that it would be in the best interests of my health to defer my acting studies altogether.

⚘

There is an infinite list of things I want to do after my transplant, but before I'm physically well enough, all I want to do is flee – preferably interstate or overseas to a place where I am no-one. I've always wanted to dance in a string bikini on a beach in Zanzibar, drinking sangria, which remains a lifelong fantasy; or get lost in the night markets in Marrakech; or eat my body weight in pizza in Italy while I take a lover and write a book. Even a few months deep into a Tasmanian winter would do. I once had a friend offer up his house, but there is too much going on for me to get away.

When it comes to my health, nothing is ever simple. I have become a stranger to myself and need to find out who I am. But with no income, thrice-weekly clinic appointments, infusions, and blood tests several times a week, the single hardest thing for a person like me to do is disappear. I want to begin again, like a baby fresh out of the womb. I may have a new, upcycled physical body, but my mind is a grease trap, and bringing myself to a point of stillness is proving impossible. My body had become a living document of pain that has been prodded, pierced, bruised and sliced into. A transplant is a radical intrusion, and I felt out of step with time. I never mention this to anyone because I feel it would come off as sounding reckless and selfish.

⚘

Around six months after my transplant, I'm hauled into clinic one day to see Scott and my surgeon, Doctor Tam.

'We think you might be addicted to morphine.'

'Okay.' I didn't *think* I was addicted to morphine. I *knew* I was.

'What we'll do is, we'll bring you in and do a slow detox over a couple of weeks.'

'Okay,' I say.

When I get home I pour my morphine down the sink. Over the years I detox cold turkey and the playbook is comparatively generic. My body aches – not in a getting-the-flu kind of way – my whole body hurts like I've been beaten in a bare-knuckle cage fight. Every fibre and every cell aflame. My legs become pistons, kicking violently into the air – across, up and out – as though they're trying to throw themselves clean from my body, much like a crab can throw its own claw. There is vomiting, shitting, shaking, sweating. Slippery as an eel, my hair is grafted to my scalp and I consider plunging my fist into a garbage disposal because it would be less painful. Of the billions of nerves in the human body, each one is white hot. I know what swallowing a bellyful of hungry, teething puppies feels like. I want to climb out of my own skin, and so I try.

This goes on for days until I slowly wend my way back into the world of the living, much like a newborn calf. After faltering on my mulish feet, I invite myself back into my body and resurface. If

I can name a time when I feel like I am back in my body, it's when I go skydiving a few years later, and the following roars through my head: *Am I about to die?*

Yes – or rather, it was easy to accept I might die jumping out of a plane.

Will I be able to breathe during free fall?

No. I felt like I was suffocating.

Was I at a place of peace after being yanked up through the air and flying like an eagle across the thermals?

Yes.

I'd been through it before – the fear, the violence, the peace, the pain. There seemed to be infinite parallels between skydiving and my transplant, except this time my mum was able to do it with me, and she was adamant that she jump first.

⚘

While I love people, I need time to decompress. I'm a creature of solitude and I attribute this duality to growing up in hospital where I was either surrounded by people or on my own – especially when in isolation in the infectious diseases ward – which set me up to derive joy out of both worlds.

In the days following my release from hospital after the transplant, I'm afraid to go out. Being one minute late to take my medication is cause for great anxiety and I enter into a hypervigilant state where everything feels like a threat to my life. If there's someone coughing or sneezing near me, instead of seeing a human all I see is a germ factory. Toddlers with snotty noses? Harbourers of disease and death. The first time I go out to dinner, someone is smoking at a nearby table, and I have a panic attack. It's the nineties, and most of my friends smoke. Everyone except my mum was smoking the night of my transplant, but they were always so careful to make sure the smoke was as far away from me as possible. My parents' devotion to nicotine prompted them to install an extraction fan above the kitchen table, so they could sit and smoke as they sipped their Nescafé Blend 43. They even put in bi-fold doors between the kitchen and the TV room to protect me from their second-hand smoke.

It takes a couple of years for my hypervigilance to abate. I'm more frightened of living than dying. Yet, I also feel a great sense of urgency because I know I'm on borrowed time. I hear stories of transplant recipients waking up and breathing unencumbered, but this has no bearing on my own experience. My brain tells me to breathe, but my body won't follow a simple command. With the advent of social media, I saw videos of people being extubated, beaming as they breathe in lungfuls of air. When you have a transplant people are under the impression, and have the expectation, that you will feel like a new person. Instead, I have to lie and tell people I feel great, instead of, 'I still can't breathe, everything is fucked.' It wasn't a new beginning. It was a deathly pause, a long exhalation. Every breath was forged in the fires of agony. I also feel indignant; frustrated I haven't had the same experience as everyone else. I wait to feel elated about breathing with new lungs, but it never comes. I don't feel twenty-one. I feel like an old woman who has had her chest bones shattered and rearranged by a toddler with a tube of araldite.

I feel alive and I feel destroyed. I do not feel broken because broken is a temporary state of being – one can always be put back together. I will not be the phoenix I had hoped to be. I will not rise. Instead, I am reduced to limping around the old ward that teems with cockroaches and a collective memory of devastation for so many families whose loved ones didn't survive. Years later I would come to understand that before I could rise from the dead I needed to spend a few days in hell.

Over the years, a faint memory – of surgeons pushing through skin, muscle and fascia, and cutting through the strata of my chest until they strike bone – grows into something more tangible. I imagine a dull sound, much like hitting bedrock with a shovel. I consider all the lives my surgeon, Dr Tam, has literally held in his hands; how he lowered his gloved hands into my chest cavity to place my new lungs. There are nights when I still wake with my palm instinctively on my sternum. My scar stretches the breadth of my chest, rising in the middle as though in prayer, and though it might be pale, after twelve years I am still pulling out little shoots of suture as they worm their way up and out through my skin. What happens in our lives writes itself into our flesh. There is wisdom in the body – a deep wisdom that beats its way through your blood.

The body remembers.

NOT LONG AFTER I RETURN home permanently, Mum drags a seemingly unwilling Dad out of the house.

'We'll be gone for a while,' she says, grabbing her handbag.

'What?' replies Dad.

'Put your shoes on, Ross. I said we'll be gone for *a while.* Come on.'

Ollie and I are lying on my bed, and as my parents drive away, I say, 'Let's have sex.'

'Your wish is my command.'

'You have to be *really* gentle.'

'I am gentle.'

'I know, but it's not going to be really rigorous fucking like it was before,' I explain with hand signals.

'What're you doing?'

'What?'

'With your hands?'

'I don't know. Just don't fuck me so hard that I burst my stitches or rebreak my sternum.'

And it is gentle. I'm still in inhumane amounts of pain, and I can't pretzel my body into the Kama Sutra like I used to, so we try different – but banal – positions until we find one where I'm not in agony. Although my sex drive isn't what it used to be by a long shot, I'm just relieved I don't injure myself.

Later, I'm talking to Mum in the kitchen.

'Well, we did it.'

'Oh, I was so hoping you would! That's why I took your father out.'

'I swear you're psychic.'

'Was it okay?'

'It was ... different from what we're used to.'

'Different how?

'Less ... frenetic,' I say, with hand signals.

'What're you doing with your hands?'

'Maybe my donor was Italian?'

⚘

On my twenty-second birthday – a year to the day since I got together with Ollie – I break it off. I seem to be perennially cranky with him, my libido has left my body, and every time I look in the mirror I cry at my chipmunk cheeks. I have another party that night with many of my friends who were with me the night of my transplant. It rains the entire evening, everyone gets uproariously drunk, and I spend the evening thinking about this time the previous year – trying to not focus on the difference one year has made to my body, for better or worse. Regrettably, I pash several friends. Regrettable because someone's tuna pasta bake had made its way into my mouth moments earlier. My friends Luke and Dean dry-retch, and my friend Shae finds my dildo and shoves it down her top.

'You have amazing tits,' I say.

'Carls, it's not working.'

'Here, let me see.'

I unscrew the cap and the rusted batteries fall out onto my bed.

'Yeah . . . it's been a while.' I laugh.

Shae grabs it and walks back to the party with it down her top like some sort of cleavage breaker.

Even though we break up, Ollie and I spend nearly every day together for the next fifteen months. We've broken up, but we haven't. I often wake up in the early hours of the morning to a 'tap-tap-tap' on my window and hear, 'Carls, it's me!' and there he is wearing his cute drunk grin. Over the years, we occasionally get together, which excites people because they think we're rekindling our romance. On these occasions, we hark back to nights eating Macca's on his bed – the difference being that now I can eat all of my food and keep it down. Ollie is kind, funny and familiar, and I still count him as one of my dear friends.

I break off our relationship because I don't know who I am or how to be in the world. The overwhelming guilt and physical pain feel like any evidence of my old life has been taken from me – as if it was ripped out of my body and dumped into the same plastic bucket as my old, black lungs.

At my twenty-year Transplanniversary party, friends say how trippy it is seeing us side by side all these years later. What we have is rare. Ollie was with me through the most tumultuous time of my life – and his. When he could have said, 'Nope – this is too hard', he stayed. He held the course and was there when the backbeat faded. He saw me lashed to fear as death chased me down, and still, he stayed. We were an exercise in patience for one another, but we were all wet-thighed and red-lipped surrender, fast food, late nights, later mornings, Nick Cave and threads of blood. I like to think I'd have been just as courageous at that age – staying with a partner who is both mad as a circus cat and probably going to die, then seeing them on life support and watching them transform into someone almost unrecognisable. Balls. Balls. Balls.

Our relationship was minted with a wicked soundtrack: Billie Holiday, Ella Fitzgerald, Nina Simone, Nick Cave and cocktail lounge music. We both recall the months leading up to the transplant, when we waltzed to 'Desiderata' outside emergency in the empty ambulance bay as it blasted out of Toby's car.

When I was on life support and in between worlds, I dreamt about waking up during surgery. I dreamt about meeting my dead friends in a world stained with yellow and pink and purple and blue. Then I heard Ella Fitzgerald and Billie Holiday. That was Ollie, who had gently put some headphones in my ears to play a mixtape he'd made. Ten years later, my sister will do the same when I'm in a coma, but not even Axl Rose can rouse me.

Human beings are born into a never-ending cycle of grief. We all traverse this landscape, and it's often expected that we will heal from every loss we experience. But what if we don't heal? In the context of illness, what happens when there is no remission and no cure? What do we do when we don't get better?

It's possible to feel grief over just about anything: people, relationships, body parts, identity, pieces of ourselves (like my vocal cord) that we lose and never find again. When I went into theatre for my transplant, I was mourning so much – my life, mainly, but there'd been a slew of things I'd lost when I was on the list. My mobility, freedom, independence; my mind and sense of self. While these might individually seem like small brutalities, together they add up. It seemed to me that, even in its most granular detail, life could change at any second.

After my surgery, I physically ache to be who I was. My bones stubbornly refuse to heal, and my mind splinters off into compartments so I can cope.

In The Transplant Diaries my mum writes: *Carly wishes she hadn't had the transplant.*

On some days, that is true. This may not be what people want to hear, but there is an all-consuming sense of guilt that I do not feel elated to be alive.

I NEVER REALISE HOW VAIN I am until I start to get fat. And when I say fat, I mean *really* fat. Or at least, really fat for me. I was wheeled into surgery weighing just shy of forty kilograms on my five-foot-three-inch frame. By the middle of 1999 I had ballooned to nearly eighty kilograms, essentially doubling my weight. Because of the colossal doses of methylprednisolone, for the first eighteen months post-surgery I am constantly ravenous.

Steroids affect your metabolism and mood and change the way your body deposits fat. When a body is sick, it's in a constant state of flux and stress, and I was burning calories just by breathing.

Not long after my transplant, I run into a girl I went to high school with, and she doesn't recognise me. In fact, she has to do a triple-take, and it's at this point that I realise I'm unrecognisable – to myself and everyone around me – and I withdraw into a state of total disconnection from the world.

I can't stop eating and I can't stop gaining weight.

Even when I'm full, my brain is screaming, 'Eat more. You can eat MORE.'

And so I do. I eat until I look like I'm in my third trimester of pregnancy. My parents' grocery bill skyrockets because of my passionate relationship with food. It's as though I'm making up for lost eating time. My head looks like I've reached up into the night sky, pulled down the moon and overlaid my face with it; my trunk is thick with an uncomfortable shelf of fluid and fat. Stretch marks traverse my belly, legs and arms like fleshy road maps. My left underarm is so deeply pocked that it looks like I've been burnt and there are deep furrows of flesh that never fill out, even when I return to a healthy weight.

After all I had endured, I never thought it would be vanity that would prove so difficult to reconcile with.

Let's look at the female body and consider the widely held view that from a primal perspective humans prefer symmetrical, evenly balanced features. While my face might be symmetrical and reasonably balanced, my insides were a mess.

A simple scientific explanation seems sound: disease and stress during childhood subtly influence the body's development. In my case, recurrent lung infections, high temperatures and never-ending courses of oral and intravenous antibiotics led to discoloured and stunted teeth. And while they were never horrible, I was never happy with them. When I ask our elderly family dentist about having my teeth whitened, he responds with, 'Nonsense – your teeth are fine.' I find another dentist and have very natural, non-Hollywood white veneers put on my top six teeth – the single best thing I've ever done for my self-esteem.

A few years later, I'm on the dance floor of my favourite nightclub, The Beat, foolishly drinking out of a bottle, when I'm tackled by a drag queen. While I'm fine, they are hysterical and insist on escorting me to the bathroom to assess the damage. One of my veneers has a chip on its corner, and the queen thinks they've maimed me for life. I give them a cuddle, tell them not to worry, take their hand and walk us back out onto the dance floor where we have a boogie. The next morning, I show Dad.

'Check it,' I say, pointing to my chipped tooth.

'I like it. Gives you more character. They look less perfect. Perfect just isn't normal.'

I never get the tooth fixed.

⸸

In November 1999 I'm at my peak weight when my parents take me on a holiday to New Zealand, which proves to be a comedy of errors. Queenstown floods for the first time in one hundred years, we don't get to see nearly enough sights, and I get sick. Perhaps worst of all is the first night when I step out of the shower. As I look at my body in the mirror, I can see vermilion-coloured welts that have bloomed all over my bottom, thighs and stomach. Initially, I think I'm bleeding, and I scream out to Mum. She rushes into the bathroom to find a hysterical me sitting in an empty bathtub. I cry and cry and cry over these new stretchmarks. As always, Mum is an angel, and instead of calling me vain or unappreciative, she draws me a bath and makes me a cup of tea.

I feel a heady sense of self-hatred that Mum and Dad's trip hasn't been the break they so deserved. Instead of sight-seeing, we're holed up in a hotel, and I try to fend off a cold. It just doesn't seem fair after all they have sacrificed for me; not just since the transplant, but for the preceding twenty-two years. They have given up everything to prolong my life, and I think the least the universe can do is give them a fucking rest.

My first solo trip to Melbourne doesn't fare much better. I spend most of the first night on the floor of my friend's toilet in agony, vomiting, not wanting to wake them up. When Alex finds me around 2 am, her and Mike rush me to The Alfred. My condition improves and I'm discharged, but I am back in hospital the next day. It's another bowel obstruction. Then, on the day I go to meet my school friend Tammy, I lose the ring that my parents had made for my twenty-first birthday. I'm wearing gloves and my fingers have shrunk from the cold, and the ring drops into a gutter in the city. The ring was a bridge between my pre- and post-transplant self, and I am heartbroken. After I'm rushed back to emergency and admitted into hospital, Mum flies down to be with me.

I am furious. I feel betrayed by my body. This is the kind of rage I am used to – the 'I'm letting other people down' rage. Even now, I still cry about what this disease took from my family.

IN THE YEAR BEFORE MY transplant surgery, my dear friend Sharon calls to ask if I'd consider being photographed by her friend, a fellow photography student.

'She's interested in capturing your journey to transplant.'

'If it happens,' I scoff. I had never been shy of a camera, and although I would be more of a subject than a model, I thought photos of me dying might open up conversations about why we're so averse to death.

'Oh shoosh. It will happen,' Sharon says, reassuringly.

I first meet Alicia on a muggy January day. A tiny Balinese woman who you could pick up and put in your pocket, she arrives with her toddler son and a lopsided haircut.

'You have amazing hair,' I say, wanting to run my fingers through the corkscrews that spring out of her head.

'Oh, I was hoping you wouldn't notice ...'

'Notice what?'

'Well ... this is a bit embarrassing, but last night my husband and I had some wine, and we thought it'd be a good idea to cut my hair.'

'I love it! It's edgy.'

'That's one word for it.' We both laugh and she spends the afternoon taking her first photos of me. We talk for a while, and it turns out Alicia is an intensive care nurse working part-time while she finishes her photography degree. I instantly fall in love with her, her husband and her children, and we grow close. She wants to capture the path to transplant for her final assessment at the Queensland College of Art. While we don't explicitly say it, we agree she would provide a visual record of either my transplant or death. I'm grateful when she doesn't extend platitudes like, 'You'll get lungs.' Because as much as hope had always loomed large in my life, I had very real expectations that I wouldn't.

Having a medical background, Alicia is practical and realistic about what might come to pass. In the months after we meet she photographs me dancing on tables, and follows me to parties, transplant clinics and outings, as well as hospital admissions – never knowing what was going to happen. We sign legal waivers with the hospital because I want her in the operating room should I have surgery: what would be the point in chronicling everything else if she didn't get to photograph my open chest? Whatever happened, Alicia was either going to capture my death or my return to life.

When I'm transferred from the Mater to The Prince Charles Hospital the night I get the call, Alicia is one of the first faces I see. I'm used to her warm presence, with her camera slung over her shoulder, and while I don't remember her joining me in theatre (she was probably being prepped), she tells me afterwards that the surgeons were more than happy to move so she could get the perfect shot. This initially horrifies me.

'So, they just moved when you asked them to?'

'Well, they would ask me if I wanted to take a photo at different times, so I snapped as many pictures as I could.'

As part of her photo documentary, Alicia isn't allowed to use a flash, so it still amazes me that she was able to capture the images she did. There are photos of my open chest, my old lungs in a bucket, what looks like my breasts being peeled over my head, and me being sewn up for the first time. 'They took such delicate care,' she says. Instinctively, she captures the exact moment my surgeon realises I'm bleeding internally and need to go back to theatre. The concern on the doctor's face is palpable, but the thing that undoes me every time I see that photo is when I see a nurse holding my hand. I might be in an induced coma, but she's holding my hand with such tenderness.

Earlier, for my own curiosity, I'd told Alicia if – on the rare chance she should find out any information about my donor – she was more than welcome to tell me.

'I mean, what are the chances of my donor ending up in your ICU?' I say months before. We both agree that it would be a one in a million coincidence.

The day after I am extubated (taken off life support), she shows me the proof sheets of my surgery. I throw up, just missing the spread of proofs in my lap. The photo of my dead lungs looks like they are dripping in nicotine. I initially think the dark colour is just the light, but Alicia assures me my 'native' lungs were black. I consider the stench – a hybrid of rotting oysters and sewage – after being stored inside this vessel, my body, for twenty-one years.

On the day I see the proofs, I clumsily broach the topic of my donor.

'I'm sorry if asking you this puts you in a terrible position.'

'It doesn't – I told you that I'd let you know if I knew anything.'

Alicia knew that my donor had died in the ICU she worked in. I ask the rudimentary questions, which immediately feel invasive.

'Was it a man or a woman?'

'A woman.'

'Younger or older?'

'She was in her twenties.'

'Oh my god. That's so young.'

'It is.'

Then I ask the inevitable question: 'Do you know what happened?'

'She had a catastrophic brain bleed.'

I'd not been expecting any information, let alone the triumvirate of gender, age and cause of death.

'Her family donated everything.'

I cry for the rest of the day, somehow feeling complicit in my donor's death. Mum and Nikki are just as emotional, and while my typically stoic dad keeps his emotions in check, I know him and 'greatly affected' would be an understatement.

The day Alicia tells me about my donor, I begin making mental notes of what I want to write in my first thank you letter. Transplant recipients are encouraged to write to their donor families, and I am eager to write a letter of my own. I know it will be censored of any identifying information because it's nationally mandated that the donation process remains anonymous. I'd heard about recipients writing in code to their donor families, with the family eventually working out who they were. Sometimes they even meet, become close friends, have barbecues and go to the beach together.

But I also knew that things could go awry. I had heard stories about donor families becoming unhealthily preoccupied with the person who's received their loved one's organs, and it's well documented that there is a risk of unhealthy relationships developing. I never think about writing in code – all I want to say is thank you. But how do you thank someone for saving your life? When I start writing, it is like turning on a tap, yet every word feels thoroughly inadequate.

What looms in my mind is that it's not about me. There were likely several people writing to give thanks after this family made an impossible decision when their young daughter was lying brain-dead in ICU. I never expect to hear back, but I still send letters.

In my first letter, I thank my donor family and acknowledge that thanking them will never be enough. I tell them a little about how I couldn't walk or shower myself before my transplant, and of my plans for the future; that they had given my family and me a reason to hope. But committing this to paper seems at odds with the sorrow I feel at the loss of their daughter, which I know was sudden and brutal. It almost seems like an exercise in cruelty.

Here I am. I am alive – your daughter is not.

I imagine the dreams they had for her – following her passions, getting an education, being happily married, having children and living a full life. I think about the dreams my parents had for me, but theirs were different from the dreams of most parents. All they ever wanted was to keep me alive, for me to survive and be happy.

Despite feeling guilty about having lived, I tell my donor family that I want to study English literature at university and travel to Spain and Morocco. I tell them about my parents and sister, and how grateful they are that I survived. Another thing that lingers in the back of my mind was that my donor family might know who I am. I had been in the newspaper numerous times both before and after my transplant, and the date and year of my surgery had been published. I'd been on television, spoken at donor thanksgiving services, and done other media.

As time passes, I selfishly hope they know who I am, that they know I've tried to make something of my life, which would not have been possible without their ultimate act of love.

Then one day, I learn my donor family have moved with no forwarding address. They are selfless and Christian – good people – and I respect that they were trying to continue with their lives while still lamenting the death of their daughter.

The only thing I know with one hundred per cent certainty is that I will be atoning for surviving for the rest of my life. I know this may not be what people want to hear because it doesn't fit the 'happily ever after' narrative. It might be an uncomfortable truth, but it is mine.

⸙

When my family and I go to Alicia's photography exhibition at the end of 1998 there are four blown-up photos of my transplant, with a book of smaller photographs she has carefully curated. Alicia asks me just before her exhibition if I've written anything about my transplant, so I whip up a poem in ten minutes, which I find printed in the book after her foreword and acknowledgements.

I find out she has been awarded top marks for her photo documentary. I'm drawn back to the corner of the room that feature the photos of me. People looking at the photos don't make the connection it's me because I'm so puffy from steroids.

'Holy shit! Is that her open chest?' I overhear.

'Yeah. That ... that's me,' I say. I'm embarrassed to draw attention to myself, but the photos give me a jolt of pride.

'That's *you*?'

I nod.

'Fucking wow!'

We have conversations about organ donation, and they are astounded that I am standing in front of them to tell the tale. For my twenty-second birthday, Alicia gifts me a book of her photos, as well as a raft of proofs and photos she experimented on in different colours. Whenever I look at them, I know it's me, but sometimes it feels like I'm looking at the intimate experience of a stranger. I am not dissociated. I am here, in the present. And yet I still find it hard to believe it's my body on that operating table, my chest open, literally off my tits (or rather, my tits are off me), about to have my sternum cracked, my chest cavity reached into and emptied. To be remade. Reborn.

DIABETES SURGES ITS WAY INTO my body after my transplant and while it's caused by a confluence of factors – the unprecedented doses of steroids I had when I was in rejection, as well as my poor CF pancreatic function – I'm curious to know if this diagnosis is connected to the fact that my body was drowning in cortisol.

In 2000, Mum and I are standing outside a church after my friend Amy's funeral when I drop dead. My legs drop out from underneath me. But before they do I remember touching Mum's arm and saying, 'I think I'm going to …'

Mercifully, Amy's family doesn't see the kerfuffle.

As my lump of a body hits the searing February asphalt, Mum assumes I'm having a hypo (severe low blood sugar). A kind lady offers some jellybeans and juice, but to Mum's horror, I am blue. She can't see my chest rising and falling and my jaw is clenched shut. Always composed, she tries to prise my jaw apart to pour some juice into my mouth. When that fails, she rubs my sternum with her knuckles and calmly calls out my name. After a few raps on my sternum, I come to.

Shoving some jellybeans into my mouth, she says, 'You weren't breathing.'

'What?'

'I think you were dead for a second.'

I try to sit up and pass out again.

There is a medical centre across the road, and the ladies from White Lady Funerals procure a wheelchair and stand in the middle of the busy road redirecting traffic as I'm ferried across their virginal blockade. I'm put into a room where a doctor takes my temperature, measures my blood glucose and oxygen saturations, all of which are stable. My blood pressure is another matter.

'I'm concerned about your high BP,' he says.

'Really, I'm fine,' I say over and over to the doctor. 'I'm sure it's nothing.'

Whatever is happening, I push it deep down, telling myself, 'You're fine. You're not dead. Because you are not dead, you're okay.'

I ask them to not call an ambulance and insist that Mum will take me to the hospital. After about an hour, they let me go at my behest and Mum takes me home.

'Are you sure we shouldn't just swing by the hospital?' she asks.

'I'm feeling much better,' I lie. What I'm most concerned about is picking up my pre-ordered copy of Seamus Heaney's translation of *Beowulf* the following day.

When Mum drives me across town to Riverbend Books to pick up the book, I see Amy's parents having a coffee. They ask how I am, and I tell them I'm fine. We talk about how beautiful Amy looked in her coffin the day before, then I hug them, and Mum and I go home. That afternoon, I'm rushed to hospital with Heaney's tome under my arm.

After a blitzkrieg of tests, I'm diagnosed as being in the midst of an Addisonian crisis. My adrenal gland is fatigued to the point of no return and my body lays crumpled in my bed, defeated.

With my new lungs, physically I have been made whole, and yet as I lie in my hospital bed, the word that springs to mind is 'broken' – bodily, existentially, psychologically and spiritually.

In hindsight, my appetite had tapered off quite sharply and I assumed it was plateauing because I was on such a low dose of steroids. I stay in hospital for a couple of days on bed rest and tear through the Heaney. It's no surprise I collapsed with adrenal fatigue – it's just miraculous it didn't happen sooner. When I find out that the cause of my Addisonian crisis is a response to physical trauma and severe stress, a million pennies drop.

I'm fat, but it's not that I can't live with the extra padding. Yes, it's uncomfortable and unfamiliar. By early afternoon, my legs swell to twice their size and my shins ache from fluid retention, but if there's one thing I find hard to grapple with, it's the size of my face. I might be able to cover my body, but my face is impossible to conceal. No matter who you are or how high your self-esteem or self-worth is, everyone struggles with moon face. When I leave hospital, I resemble a toffee apple – fat head, skinny body. I liken my appearance to a chipmunk: tiny little eyes that disappear into my face when I smile.

As for my scars, they are stories of survival, and for that, I love them. What once looked like crucifixes from chest drains now look more akin to star bursts. Markings from the insertion and removal of ports in my chest and abdomen, as well as central lines in my neck and chest, that once had my skin looking like the surface of the moon have faded.

Some people say they don't remember what their body looked like before they had the scars. I do. My skin was flawless, my breasts piled high on my chest with no marks scored on the flesh running beneath them. My transplant scar stretches the breadth of my chest, under my breasts and ending at my side ribs. It really does look like I've been cut in half, but now the scar is barely visible.

All of these scars have made a home on my body, providing a timeline of sorts, and sometimes even a sign of hope for others.

But more than this, my scar connects me to a person I'll never meet, and so my story is not wholly my own.

⚘

When I was in my twenties I didn't really understand the different ways that stress can impact health. After all, the biggest issues my peers were having at the time were sitting uni exams, staying employed and paying rent. Looking back, I can see I've been dealing with more than my fair share of stress my whole life. Trauma psychiatrist Judith Herman cites hyper-arousal, intrusion and constriction as the three main symptoms of PTSD. Hyper-arousal can manifest as irritability, engaging in impulsive and risk-taking behaviours, hypervigilance, sleep disturbances and psychosomatic complaints. What I have from that list is hypervigilance and uncontrollable insomnia.

Hypervigilance is mostly associated with war veterans and is clinically defined as a heightened sense of alertness with behaviours that endeavour to prevent danger. When experiencing hypervigilance your subconscious is perpetually anticipating danger and so your senses are on high alert, ready to respond to a threat. There is a series of physical and behavioural symptoms and every person experiencing hypervigilance has a different trajectory. For me, physical symptoms would present as a rapid heartbeat or sweating, although people have asked if I'm high because my pupils constrict to tiny pinpoints of black. As a mistress of adaptation from a young age I have learnt how to hide my hypervigilance. As a child, it was as though I wore a mask. Ever the actress, I always pretended that everything was fine, even when it was far from it. This is something I continue to use in my adult life, knowing it makes everyone else feel better if I don't look or act upset.

My behavioural symptoms, on the other hand, are ever changing. When I'm in a movie theatre I make a mental note of the exit signs before the movie starts so I can calculate how long it will take to get out if there's a fire or if someone starts shooting into the dark. I like to sit up the back with a clear view of both sides so no-one can come up from behind and surprise me. But the fire could start up the back, so I do a quick headcount of how many people are in the theatre to see how many I could save on the way out. Like a war veteran, I like to sit where I can see the front door. You can't miss what you can see coming. Noisy and overcrowded places can be cause for overwhelm. I don't enjoy shopping centres – I'm happier at an outdoor market where I can feel the air and the sun on my skin.

I've tried to condition (read: force) myself to sit where I can't see an escape route, but instead of neutralising the apparent threat, I'll silently catastrophise. Over time, I've learnt to sit with the discomfort as I attempt to retrain my brain to not think of the worst possible outcome. After a lifetime of having pain foisted upon me – for example, waking up in the middle of the night and being held down as a needle was driven into my arm – it's not something that I can easily forget. At their core, these attempts to save me were an assault on my body. End-stage CF was like an untameable beast tearing its way through my body, and memory calls me back to that place – to my dying – frequently. There is a liminality to this time that, even though my memory has processed it millions of times, frame by frame, its lucidity is startling. It is like a fish hook I cannot and will never be able to remove from my finger. Time has this unrelenting momentum that you cannot release yourself from. You have to surrender to it, peacefully or otherwise. But it's best to let it pass through you without too much struggle. Much like dying.

As a child I rarely catastrophised, but I was always mentally prepared. If I got septicaemia, needed multiple surgeries for endometriosis, or if I had an adverse reaction to one of my medications, I tended to feel apathetic because I was used to drifting from disaster to disaster. In times of acute distress, I would find myself sizing up every potential threat. For anyone, that's exhausting. For a child, it can be all-consuming. Whenever I saw a man in a white coat coming towards me, I knew I was about to be hurt, yelled at, or both, because that's what I believed their job was. It was a typical Pavlovian response. I always felt like I was born to be broken. Everything about CF felt so punitive.

Perhaps even more punitive was my constant need to atone and overachieve, which led to my addiction to narcotics – a weakness that first sunk its teeth in when I was nineteen. After going cold turkey from morphine in 1999, I start getting migraines that need pethidine injections to get under control.

It gets to the stage where I have my own supply of injectables, and for someone like me who worshipped these kinds of drugs, I was making deals with death I knew I couldn't keep. It was a full-time job at one point, where I'd have to stagger my doses with precision. I knew what to say to my doctors to get more: variations of 'I vomited them up', 'lost the script', 'left the morphine in the car'. I'd have to steel myself to pretend I was straight, but I would have mental blanks of days and weeks. Because it had been prescribed, I deluded myself into thinking it was safe. But more people die from pharmaceutical opioid overdoses than any other drug, and these deaths far outweigh the national road toll.

At the 2004 Byron Bay Writers Festival I'm suspended in a drug bubble with a steady supply of pethidine. It proves to be far more alluring than going to listen to any writer. When the inevitable comedown begins, I snap the top off another ampoule, inject the contents into my leg and instinctively know that if there is a god – an all-loving god – then this is my version of them.

Frankenstein's monster, centaurs, minotaurs, selkies. The long list of animal/human creatures in folklore reaches back thousands of years. Humanity had been fascinated by the hybrid body long before eighteen-year-old Mary Shelley wrote her novel. As you read this, scientists are creating 'chimeras' – crosses between humans and animals. In its modern incantation, 'chimera' means illusion. In Greek mythology, a chimera is a fire-breathing hybrid composed of the parts of more than one animal, while in genetics, it means an organism that contains cells from more than one individual. Chimeras can occur naturally during development (such as when non-identical twins merge early on) or can be created through an artificial process. Technically, organ transplants create chimeras. Am I a chimera? Not quite.

In 2021, a privately funded lab in the United States created human-monkey hybrid embryos by injecting stem cells from a human foetus's skin into a monkey embryo. If implanted into a monkey uterus, this chimera could theoretically develop into a live-born animal with cells from both a monkey and a human. It might feel like a violation of the boundaries between species, but it's here, and it's happening.

While there's little to no data about the personal effects of lung transplants, heart transplant recipients have been studied widely, and there's an abundance of literature about how they're affected personally, culturally, politically and spiritually. Studies show that it's not the biomedical risk of transplantation that causes most concern, but how such procedures disrupt the recipient's image of being embodied as an individual and what transplantation can mean for personal identity.

What have I absorbed? What has been transferred? Is it possible that I now have two sets of DNA? Did I notice anything different after my transplant – a desire for foods or music I'd never liked before? The only thing I can think of is sushi. After my transplant, I ate sushi non-stop for eighteen months, but I think this had more to do with my insatiable hunger, caused by the massive doses of steroids. I was just really fucking hungry.

For a while I ruminated on the power and possibility of different thought patterns or a dual memory. Bone marrow transplant recipients are the only people who actually share DNA with their donors and medical opinion is sceptical over whether organ recipients can gain more than just a lifeline from transplants. Still, donor antibodies do meld into your system and lower immunosuppression levels. And there are numerous cases of organ donor recipients who find themselves doing things they've never done before. Preferences that parallel the donor's own have been known to occur, whether it's food, art, music, recreation, career or even sexual preferences. Could this just be a coincidence? Unfortunately, research is scarce and often hyperbolic.

After reading vastly and thinking deeply about my own experience, I believe that there can be a cellular transfer. It's a simple fact that everything – humans included – is made up of energy. Gary Schwartz, a professor of medicine, neurology, psychiatry and surgery at the University of Arizona, asserts that research by his team has found definite links. He calls it 'cellular memory'.

Schwartz documented seventy cases in which he believes transplant recipients have inherited the traits of their donors. It's essentially an exchange of energy, where what is stored in their organ is passed on to the recipient. His studies found that heart and heart-lung transplant patients are the most likely to experience personality changes, although his theory applies to any organ that has cells that are interconnected, including kidneys, liver and even muscles.

Being highly sensitive and intuitive, I did feel that there was something within me – truly within me on a cellular level – that had changed after my transplant. Not outwardly, but I felt a subtle change at the centre of my being as though there was something else within me, like my core had changed, or the essence of me had been altered. I knew there was something new within me, but I was never sure of what that was. And it felt like multiple new things, much like a human Russian nesting doll.

Much of the time, the notion of 'cellular memory' is chalked up to pseudoscience and/or a psychosomatic disorder. But for people experiencing the changes, I can attest that they are very real. I've learnt over the course of my life that there are limitations to what can and can't be explained by science and medicine. If the body remembers trauma, then it only makes sense that organs have a cellular memory.

⚘

Just before my sister's first wedding anniversary, I'm walking down the hallway when Dad hands me his phone.

'Who is it?'

'Nikki. She wants a quick word,' he says casually.

'What's up?' I ask her.

'How do you feel about being an auntie?'

'Whaaaaaaaaat?'

Dad is beaming and I'm laughing and crying.

I scream, 'When?'

'Next March.' She giggles.

'This is the best news ever! Holy shit, I'm going to be an auntie!'

'I thought you'd be keen!'

Eight months later, on 20 March 2001, I am there for the birth of her first child – a son. Nikki has gestational diabetes, which necessitates a caesarean delivery, and I'm lucky enough to be a support person and photographer. Because I love all things gore, as the surgeon guts my sister like a fish, I clandestinely move my way down her body to get a better look at muscle, blood, fat and, hopefully, an amniotic sac and placenta.

'Can I just like ... have a gander?'

'You can look,' Nikki says, 'but for god's sake, don't take any photos!'

'How is it different from seeing photos of my open chest?'

'Because it's *me*, and I'm awake!'

I have to respect that.

That afternoon, I stand in a hospital room and watch my parents cry with joy at this tiny human my sister has nurtured for nine months. His name is Timothy Brodie – Brodie being Dad's middle name. It's hard to hand him back or put him down in his cot; everything about him is perfection. His olive skin is smoother than velvet, his eyes dark as agates, baby fingers little pegs of wonder.

A few weeks later, I'm at my sister's when she has to go to the supermarket. As Tim sleeps soundly on my chest, his tiny body in a perfect loop of breath, I get the tiniest inkling of what it's like to be a mother, and in that moment I know I would die for him.

In September 2003, Daniel William arrives. The complete opposite of Tim, he comes out chunky, pale and with a shock of white hair. Mum drops the camera on the operating room floor because she's so excited and startled by his appearance.

In January 2005, Mitchell Byron arrives earth-side, and again, I'm lucky enough to be at the birth. Mitchell looks like a mini-me, with his tan skin, blonde hair, freckles and green eyes.

Then, in January 2007, when Samuel Nicholas arrives, I call it – Nikki has succeeded in building her own modelling agency. No-one has time to take any photos because Nikki goes into early labour from a stress-related event. For reasons still unknown, when Sam is seven months old, he stops eating, and my sister has to learn how to insert a nasal gastric tube up his nose and into his stomach as he screams and writhes under her hand.

'I don't know how Mum did it with you. It's the most awful thing I've ever had to do,' she cries.

Sammy's a sickly little thing, but ever so spirited. Giving birth to and raising four boys in six years is a massive undertaking for any parent, but to compound the pandemonium when Sam is three, after being in hospital for six days with asthma, he goes into respiratory arrest and dies in my sister's arms. As she nurses his body, she looks down to see his tiny chest cave in, and it takes doctors two hours to stabilise him before he's rushed to the Royal Children's Hospital across town.

As I walk in to visit Sam in ICU, I see Paul, one of my favourite nurses who used to look after me.

'Is he yours?' Paul whispers across the room.

'My nephew,' I whisper back.

'He's in good hands.'

'I know,' I say, giving him a nod and a smile.

Sam makes a full recovery, and for my sister, life continues, albeit with one very sick little boy. His asthma is an unpredictable and untameable beast. He can be screaming around the yard of a morning and be in the back of an ambulance by lunchtime. He has countless trips and admissions to hospital, and my sister says again, 'I don't know how Mum did it.'

'Me either,' I say.

Illness has been romanticised for eons, with tuberculosis (TB), or consumption, the most glamorised disease of the nineteenth century. Loaded with allegory, TB was seen as something of a moribund fashion aesthetic revered by Victorians – often weaponised by women to imply frailty – and it had a pervasive cultural impact at the time.

Women would use make-up to replicate the alabaster skin and rosy cheeks associated with consumption, as well as embellishing poor posture – a by-product of CF. Dante Rossetti's painting *Beata Beatrix* is a gauzy portrait of a woman dying of TB. It features a false equivalence of a beautiful – even graceful – death, while a watercolour by renowned death portraitist Richard Tennant Cooper depicts a young lady dying on a balcony in the countryside. She's clutching a handkerchief in one hand, as the angel of death holds the other, hovering over her with a scythe and hourglass. The reality of TB was substantially different: essentially eating you from the inside out, filling your chest cavity with blood and pieces of liquefied lung that sufferers would try to expectorate out of their mouth, but inevitably choke on.

Lord Byron had hoped that TB might make him more appealing to his lady suitors, declaring, 'How pale I look! – I should like, I think, to die of consumption … because then the women would all say, "see that poor Byron – how interesting he looks in dying!'" A paradox if ever there was one.

There's a grand romanticism surrounding illness in pop culture, particularly when it comes to cancer. My dying was hardly romantic. It was coughing up cupfuls of mucus and blood, pissing the bed, and fracturing ribs when I coughed. My dying was sucking on nitrous oxide a la Dennis Hopper in *Blue Velvet* while I was expectorated by a physio who eventually had to stop pounding my chest because of the pain that ricocheted through my trunk. I was not 'intoxicated by my illness' like Anatole Broyard in his book of the same name. There was this liminal state of being interested, but I was only interested in how I could *tame* it. More than anything, I was terrified. I had had enough of the interminable pain. My dying was passing out in the shower while on the highest flow of oxygen. My dying was losing my mobility along with my dignity. This was before the days of Bi-Pap, which is a machine where air is forced deep down into your lungs to give you a rest. I breathed every craggy breath and felt every crackle thud through my chest like slow-burning cordite.

The fetishisation of illness is on fine display in films like *Stepmom* and *The Fault in our Stars.* Recent films like *Five Feet Apart* – about CF – fail to connect. I've watched a few clips on YouTube, and frustratingly, the leads aren't nearly emaciated or breathless enough. Why are their lips not blue? Why are they not wheezing? Why aren't their contorted spines pushing through their clothing? Where are the ten-minute coughing fits where they fart and piss and shit their pants?

When I was growing up, there was one film about CF called *Alex: The Life of a Child.* Made in 1986, it's based on a true story about Alex Deford, whose father Frank was a well-known American sportswriter. Alex died in 1980 when she was nine years old. I remember the film being whispered about because word had got around to us kids that certain people didn't want us to see the film because it would be too distressing.

What didn't they want us to see in a movie that we hadn't already seen in real life? We'd seen friends bringing up cupfuls of blood. We'd been there when friends died, the curtains drawn, and us being ordered to stay on our beds as their bodies were spirited away to the morgue. It felt almost perverse that it was taboo to talk about a film. I eventually saw it after some brave soul made a VHS copy and left it in a secret place in the ward like some sort of prison contraband. Admittedly, I swore throughout the entire ending because, despite drowning in her own blood and mucus, movie Alex has the energy to sit up and speak in the moments before she dies. That's something I hadn't seen before. The other disorienting thing was that I was used to seeing Bonnie Bedelia as Bruce Willis's wife in the Christmas classic *Die Hard* and, as such, was expecting John McClane to burst into the room with an Uzi before grabbing the kid so he could whack some donor lungs in to save her life.

My friends had languished in comas for days before they died, so while this romanticism was a little maddening, I did see some stark parallels between Alex and myself. We were both total hams who refused to let CF define us, and we always wanted to make other people feel happy.

Once in a while, a marvel of a film will come along, featuring performances that resonate with my own experience, such as Isabel Coixet's study of motherhood and cancer in *My Life Without Me* and the incomparable Emma Thompson as a turgid English literature professor in *Wit*. These films are the ones I've always been drawn to. They trill with truth because they aren't afraid to show the mundanity of a prognosis.

⸙

I was never destined to be a mother in the traditional sense. Having CF can make it difficult to conceive, and I always knew that pregnancy would most likely result in my death. Women with CF who have babies tend to get very sick, very quickly. Hormones can exacerbate infections, and the baby pushes on the diaphragm, which in turn places enormous pressure on the lungs. I have had friends who died when their children were toddlers.

The other thing I learn is that it will be extra difficult for me to conceive because of severe endometriosis. However, unlike many women who find themselves unable to have children, it's something I've never mourned. I've always had far bigger losses to contend with. Growing up, I mothered the kids I was in hospital with. From the age of eight, whenever I was in the same room as a baby, I would feed them, play with them, sing to them, change their nappies and rock them to sleep. I was happy to do what the nurses often didn't have the time to do, so it was second nature to lower a cot rail when a baby was crying so I could scoop them up and settle them. Spending so much time in hospital, I also saw many children suffer.

When I was in the isolation ward in high school, I was lucky enough to share many admissions with Cindy and Sharlene, two young sisters from a country town who both had hair so blonde they had coronas of light above their heads. As the eldest, Cindy looked after Sharlene. We would hear the murderous matron yelling at us from the desk, her voice reverberating down the hall, which made us dissolve into puddles of giggles. She could be scary, but only if you let her. I often ate with the girls in their room and did my version of reading them bedtime stories. The girls knew I wrote poetry, and they asked me to read them the most disturbing poems from my battered copy of Sylvia Plath's *Ariel* I always brought into hospital with me. Then, I would tuck them into bed, kiss their foreheads, and trundle back to my room where I listened to Cindy coughing in the night. She died in 1994; Sharlene in 2006 after having had a transplant.

Even post-transplant, I don't think about whether I can be a mum or not because it's just not on my radar. There was only one man I wanted children with, and that was Marcelo. Having children is also far too risky due to the anti-rejection medication I take, and from a purely selfish perspective, I really like my sleep and have a proclivity for seafood and soft cheeses.

In 2006, I receive a phone call from my gynaecologist. I'm standing at my parents' kitchen table when she says she has bad news, and I immediately deduce I have cervical cancer. While the abnormal growth of cells in my cervix is high, there's a far more pressing matter: there are dysplastic (pre-cancerous) changes on my vulva, and so she refers me to a gynaecological oncologist (there is such a specialty – *A broken box doctor?*, I thought). For twelve months, we try to keep the pre-cancer in situ with non-invasive treatments and as little excision surgery as possible, of which, in the end, there is a lot. And by non-invasive treatments, I mean ointments that melt the skin off my vulva.

If you've had a basal cell carcinoma, you would know about Efudix. Every day, I snap on surgical-grade gloves and paint on the topical chemotherapy. It essentially melts cancer cells away, which is tremendous if you have skin cancer on your arm or your face. Not nearly as delightful if you have it on your vulva. Within a fortnight, my vulva is peeling, the skin bleeding and tearing off in chunks. Going to the toilet is an exercise in agony, and as more skin tears away, there is more pain and a greater need for opioids. By the time it's decided that the topical chemotherapy isn't working, my vulva resembles minced meat.

The cancer, as I can see it, is palpable and visual: discolouration of the skin, going from a blushing pink to a dove grey. There are visible lumps, and should my oncologist so desire, he could draw a dot-to-dot, making a cunt constellation. The physicality of my disease has never aggressively shown itself, but the cancer has colonised my entire vulva and my entire perineum. People talk of the irony of cancer, but the irony is that there is no irony. Cancer is such a cliché, and sickness has a way of making people seem less banal and far more interesting than they actually are. If anything, cancer turns out to be incredibly mundane. Painful, but mundane. Mutilating, but mundane.

In 2007, the vulval dysplasia I have is rapidly turning into cancer. After eighteen months of skin-peeling ointments and surgery, it's clear I need major surgical intervention. I'm not shocked or particularly worried because I'm on doses of OxyContin that would sedate an elephant. In October, I face the biting force of reality when I'm told that to survive I need to have a 'skinning' or 'radical' vulvectomy. In layman's terms, surgeons will cut and peel the skin away from the tip of my clitoris to the top of my rectum, which will require extensive skin grafting. I am told it is 'very serious', to which I say, 'Wait – I have *cunt cancer*?' and laugh like a maniac. I don't think my doctor has ever seen a patient have that reaction, but laughing at a cancer diagnosis is so very me.

As it turns out, it's no laughing matter. Being immuno-suppressed and diabetic, there is every chance the skin grafts won't take.

Before my surgery, my parents and I head up to the Sunshine Coast for some respite. We have a few days of peace, with walks along the beach and lunch with two of my mainstays, Bec and Dylan, and their new baby boy. Mid-week, I have to come back for an appointment with my oncologist and the plastic surgery team. The surgery is going ahead despite my transplant consultant telling me I need to think seriously about not going through with it. But I am well and truly dwelling in the kingdom of zero options, and my oncologist says, 'This isn't just about preserving your womanhood. It's about saving your life, Carly.'

On this day, Dad drives Mum and me down to the hospital and into a day neither of us is expecting. By the time we see the plastic surgeon, it's closing in on 5.00 pm. Afterwards, as we wait for my OxyContin prescription, we're both in tears over what we've just been told, and the pharmacist is snappy, as though she's angry with me because she is still there after five o'clock.

The conversation with the plastic surgeon had gone something like this:

'We're going to have to take all of the skin off.'

Skin off. Is that like the movie, Face Off?

'We'll need to redirect your bowel, so you'll have an ileostomy for at least three months.'

A poo bag.

'If you don't have an ileostomy, you'll die from infection.'

I'll die.

'We need to remove all the skin.'

You already said that.

'We will take the skin from your inner thigh.'

I'm going to be walking around with part of my thigh on my vulva.

'Because you're immunosuppressed and diabetic, there's a high risk of the graft not taking, so we might have to get you back into surgery so we can take more skin and re-graft the site.'

More skin.

'This is what we will do.'

Ah, Doctor. You're not the most subtle news breaker.

⚘

Much to my parents' horror, I feel the need to reclaim my womanhood before it's cut away, so I throw a 'pre-designer vagina' party. Friends walk into a pub armed with phallic balloons and wind-up penis toys that we have races with across the bar. They throw crotchless knickers at me – like the hen's party I'd never had – and I'm upbeat, levitating on a cloud of OxyContin and half a bottle of gin.

Not long before surgery, my transplant consultant, Peter, wants to see me.

'I really don't know about this surgery, mate. It could kill you.'

'Pete, I haven't come this far so that cancer can kill me. I'm going to throw whatever I can at it. Seriously, what a horrible way to go.'

I felt hamstrung. It was the first time I'd not followed Pete's advice. He had been looking after me before my transplant, and our relationship had been forged in the fires of joy and grief.

I'm admitted into hospital the day before my surgery so I can meet the stomal therapy nurses. Two fabulous women are looking after me. Val has a short crop of silver hair and skin so olive her teeth glow, while Lizzie is a young, dizzyingly beautiful blonde. Their patience and kindness in the coming weeks and months will bring me undone every time I see them.

'We're in this together,' Lizzie says as she draws a daisy on my belly where the ileostomy is going to be. I like the flower. I want the flower to stay because it looks fitting beside the rainbow tattoo I'd had inked on my belly when I was nineteen. But mostly, I want the flower to stay because I don't want to look down and see part of my exposed bowel jutting out of my stomach. One misplaced fear is that the aesthetic of my tattoo is going to be drastically altered.

The night before the surgery, I have to do what's called a 'bowel evacuation'. It's essentially an inverse enema where one drinks several litres of a solution that tastes like pool water – much like the stuff I drank to clear bowel obstructions when I was a kid. In turn it makes you shit your guts out, so your bowel is 'clear' for surgery. I drink while my sister and I text late into the night as I evacuate my bowel. I ask for a dose of OxyContin for my pain, but it's really to blunt my fear.

'How are you even conscious?' the nurse asks me.

I shrug my shoulders. 'My threshold for opioids is exceptional,' I say, smiling.

'It certainly is. You're in pretty good spirits.'

Another thing I do is watch Chris Lilley's *Summer Heights High*, which, coupled with the bowel prep, has me shitting myself laughing – an effective method of bowel evacuation if ever there was one. My closest friends message me with the gloomiest edge of humour because they know I can take it. There are some vulgar conversations, and I savour every single one.

All night, I run my hand over the smooth skin where a bag will swing from for the next three months. When I wake up the next morning, my hand instinctively goes to my belly, which is, as yet, untouched. It's one of the only places on my body where I've never had a scar, and it's quite beautiful. Soft and flat; pale as porcelain.

After having a shower with the disinfectant pre-surgical wash, I change into a gown. When I am in the waiting room with my parents, there's a young couple holding hands, and I can tell the woman has had a miscarriage.

That poor woman, I think.

A nurse appears, which means a rushed goodbye. I hug Mum and Dad, and we exchange several 'I love you's. As I'm shuttled through to pre-op, I think, *My sister should be here*. And then, *She has four babies to look after*. And then, *But she was here for the transplant*. And finally, *Oh, this isn't that major. Wait. Is it?*

Theatre is always subarctic, and I am used to its machinations – friendly voices both hushed and loud, Velcro being prised apart on blood pressure cuffs, warm blankets being cast over bodies, beeping monitors, the clang of metal gurneys. I'm reminded of the symphony of theatre and me, an unmoving lump of flesh about to be skinned alive. There are surgeons, theatre nurses and muscle men who prep me for surgery. I'm surprised to find out it will take just as long as my transplant. Different teams move in and out, weaving around each other as though in a dance. I hadn't reconciled the magnitude of what was about to be done to my body until that morning when Rusty, my oncologist, said there's a chance he would have to remove my clitoris.

'I know you have the Hippocratic Oath to uphold, but please just leave me to die on the table. Just try to clandestinely kill me. You're a doctor – some potassium chloride should do the trick.'

'How do you even know that?' he'd asked, shaking his head, but with a smile on his face.

'Rusty, I've had an exit plan since I was fifteen.'

After I'm put to sleep, I am placed into what is called a dorsal lithotomy position, which is a medical way of saying I am on my back with my legs spread in the air. First up, the plastic surgery team cut and peel the skin from the top of my clitoris to the top of my rectum. I wonder afterwards what kind of knife they used. Electric? A Bowie knife? A combination or scalpel and cautery? They manage to preserve my clitoris, but the skin that covers it is cut away and grafted over with skin from my thigh. This involves shaving a large piece of skin off my left thigh with a dermatome – a surgical instrument used to peel thin slices of skin from the donor site. Then the skin is rolled through what looks like a pasta-making machine to make the skin mesh-like so it can be stretched and grafted onto my vulva and rectum. This is called an autologous skin graft.

With the donor skin laid out across my vulva all the way down to the top of my rectum, it's then secured into place with sutures and taped down with a dressing, as is the remaining skin on my left thigh. To create a stoma, a small part of my small intestine is pulled to the surface of my stomach and sutured into place. Ileostomies can be made with one end of the small intestine, which is how mine is fashioned. I have what is called a 'loop ileostomy', where both the upstream and downstream ends of my small intestine (the ileum) are stitched onto the surface of the skin. The reason I need to have my bowel redirected is so that the skin that's been removed from my rectum can stay clean. Disappointingly, shit isn't aseptic.

I don't remember waking up in recovery or being taken up to the ward. It's little wonder, since my body and my brain are trying to process the trauma and I am on generous doses of morphine. When I do wake up, the pain not so much takes my breath away as colonises my entire body. I've effectively been skinned, and the pain in my sex organs and my stomach – where my stoma sits above my skin like a shiny, little red mountain – is comparable to when I had my transplant.

The six-hour surgery had gone well, and Pete comes to see me the next day. He couldn't be happier with how well I look after such a long and brutal surgery. For all intents and purposes, I'm in a stable condition. He holds my hand, and I say, 'I'm not dead yet.' I can see he's teary.

Because I have a lot of friends who want to visit, my sister creates a Facebook group to keep everyone up to date with my condition. It will become something of a lifeline for them. I do remember my best friend Bec visiting me days after the operation. When she visits, I find it hard to speak or stay awake because of the levels of pain relief I am on. She sits by my bedside and cradles my hand in hers. I ask how baby Isaac is, her son who had been born on my mum's sixtieth birthday. Bec gives me a rose quartz heart that's almost the width of my palm, and I hold onto it for the rest of my stay. The stone is a perfect cloudy pink, but when I leave hospital, I notice it's heaving with fissures, with a very visible crack right down the middle. Make of that what you will.

It matters not what the pain team give me – morphine, ketamine, fentanyl. One day, while Dad is visiting, I start screaming. My hands, white-knuckled, grip the sides of the bed, the strength in my wrists pulling my body up until I am half sitting. The pain is a searing force that seizes the entirety of my lower body. It feels like someone has poured fuel over my lap and set me alight. There is a disconcerting sense of déjà vu. One night, I chew the skin off the inside of my cheeks. The brain isn't designed to protect us from pain. The body wants us to feel pain as an evolutionary response so we can escape from what is hurting us.

In a perfect confluence of events, a large obstruction forms in my bowel. I haven't been fed for days and should be on supplemental feeding. My body's electrolytes – salt, magnesium, potassium – have reached such perilously low levels that I later find out they put me in cardiac arrest territory. To say it's a monumental fuck-up is an understatement of biblical proportions. Before my surgery, there should have been a round table discussion and a post-surgical plan put in place. A crucial part of that plan should have been that I go straight from theatre to ICU. Because of my complex medical history, after such a long and complicated surgery, it's almost puerile that I'm in the broken cunt ward.

A territorial war erupts between two oncology registrars and my brilliant transplant consultant. The registrars don't want to include the transplant team because it's an oncology issue. Essentially, it's a one-sided pissing contest, but you can't afford to be territorial when you have a critically ill patient.

I ask my consultant Pete what the issue between the two teams is. 'Why do they hate you?'

'They think we're elitist.'

'Well, you are – you're looking after me.'

'This is true.' He smiles.

'I'm kidding. It sounds like a cock-measuring contest to me.'

He nods, still smiling.

Unfortunately, the edict of 'do no harm' doesn't seem to be on their radar. My stomach is so distended I look eight months pregnant. I'm taken down to radiology to have a rather invasive scan called a barium enema. I'm strapped to a table that tilts me up so that I'm vertical. The criminally good-looking radiologist injects a barium solution into my stoma, and I worry that it's going to explode shit all over him. The scan lasts for around an hour, and for the first time since my surgery, I find myself full of rage. I'm delirious from pain and lack of sleep. A man standing behind the glass is looking at my images and asking me strange questions.

'Who *is* that?' I ask.

He identifies himself as a radiologist.

I am apoplectic with rage.

'You muppet.'

'No, I'm a radiologist.'

'No, you're a MUPPET.'

The other radiologists have a giggle. I still have my sense of humour. Just as suspected, I am full of shit. That afternoon, I become aphasic and cannot speak. I'm bringing up green bile that bubbles up and out of my throat like an unrepentant volcano.

'Darling, let me know when you need the bowl,' Mum says lovingly, as my sister looks on, shocked into silence.

But I can't speak to tell anyone when it's coming, and the nurses keep having to clean me up and change my gown. I haven't thrown up since I had a surgery four years earlier to stop me aspirating into my lungs, and while I may not be able to speak, I'm lucid enough to know that if I'm throwing up, something is dreadfully wrong.

Though I don't remember it, when Dad visits me the next day, he finds me propped up on plastic hospital pillows in a recliner, drooling and slack-jawed with a thousand-yard stare. He walks out to the nurses' station to ask what's going on.

'She's just tired. She needs rest,' the nurses say.

He's not convinced I'm 'just tired'. Mum joins him, and they're both shocked by my apparent vegetative state. Not long after they go downstairs for a coffee, Dad gets a call saying they need to get back up to the ward because I'm throwing massive seizures – seizures I do not wake up from. Seizures that send me into a coma. I'm stabilised and rushed to ICU, where I have brain scans. There is talk of brain damage.

Dad calls Pete, my transplant consultant, fully aware that without his help I am going to die. Pete saves my life (on his day off, no less). Later, I hear how happy the registrars were to see him – the same doctors who had been so intent on dismissing his initial input. He orders that all pain medications be stopped, that I be put on total parenteral feeding (TPN) to give me the nutrients I need and to get my electrolytes rebalanced. Pete doesn't leave until I'm stable, and Dad goes on to buy him several bottles of very expensive wine.

Meanwhile, I'm not waking up, seemingly straddling two worlds. When I begin to wake sporadically, my legs thrash around the bed from acute narcotic withdrawal. My knees turn various shades of violet. I feel like I am either being burned alive or like my bones have been dipped in dry ice. When I am hot, I feel like I'm cooking from the inside out, and Mum and the nurses lay cool cloths and ice packs on my body, then take them away and wrap me up like a blanket burrito when I get so cold that my whole body shakes. They do this dozens of times, and I am so grateful to them.

When I am comatose, I have nightmares. This time when I wake up, I'm not terrified of living but of dying. I say to Mum, 'This feels like another transplant' and the thought of going home with an ileostomy repulses me.

When I wake up properly, I'm impervious to whatever pain there is simply because it's so thrilling to be alive. I don't even need paracetamol. Instead, I am in a frenzy of rage that I've come so close to either dying or sustaining catastrophic brain damage because one medical team didn't want to include the other; because of egos and a need to be right. I call my experience 'the cunt cancer coma'.

Plastic surgeons need to check the site twice a day to see how my skin grafts are healing on my vulva, rectum and inner left thigh. It unsettles me that all of my main clinicians are men, and it feels like my body is being colonised by the male gaze. Making things more uncomfortable is that it's November, aka Movember, and all of the younger male doctors from gynaecology and plastic surgery have moustaches; it feels like I've been thrown back in time to a 1970s porn set. The irony is not lost on me, and I'm thankful when two female doctors from plastics come to look at my vulva one afternoon.

'It's so nice to have you here instead of the guys,' I say.

I don't see another male plastics doctor for the remainder of my stay.

Because I'm the youngest person to have had this kind of cancer, I often wake up to see several strangers at the end of my bed wanting to see my mangled lady bits, including medical students and newly minted doctors. I realise that I am always sharing my body with someone else – a doctor, a physio, a nurse, another patient – and it feels like a betrayal. I hear them milling outside my room.

'This is Carly Metcalfe. Thirty years old, CF, diabetic, immunosuppressed from a lung transplant. We're just waiting for the tumour board regarding the pathology, but there was no lymph node involvement.'

A tumour board? Is this a board they pin patients' tumours on? Do they gather in some secret room in the hospital to play 'Pin the tail on the tumour'? I imagine doctors meeting in party hats and leaving with lolly bags, while pieces of flesh hang from a corkboard.

'Mind if we have a look?' they ask.

It never occurs to me to say no.

After two weeks in bed, the muscles in my legs have atrophied and I have to learn how to walk again with the help of three nurses, a wardsman and a stand-up walker. My first crossing of the hall is met with applause, and a punch of 'I've been here before'. Feeding myself and being able to walk around the ward unaided both feel like small miracles.

When cancer patients finish chemotherapy, they get to ring a chemo bell – a highly emotional release heralding a person's return to the kingdom of the well. I leave hospital after three weeks with barely a whimper. There is no chemo bell for me, no offers to debrief or suggestions for counselling. I might not have had my breasts lopped off, but I won't return to myself for some time, and again, I'll have to do it on my own. Before my surgery, I looked at support groups for women with vulva cancer, and while there was one in Brisbane, all of the women were in their sixties. The median age for vulva cancer is seventy, so there were only older women to speak with. I'm thirty and can't imagine that I have anything in common with these women except our illness.

My oncologists tell me not long after my surgery that with my levels of immunosuppression, they're concerned the cancer could be like Hydra: that they have cut off its head only for it to keep regrowing. Cunt cancer is not how I saw my dirty thirties panning out. My thirties are not supposed to be filled with fear and a bag of shit swinging off my gut.

Rosebud. That's what I call the little red volcano of my stoma. I'm tempted to stick my finger in the hole where shit spurts out just to see what will happen, but I don't want to tempt fate. What I notice when I do touch it is how smooth it feels, the way my finger glides over its slippery nub. It's glassy – almost reflective – and feels like a knob of butter.

As for the ileostomy, I don't know how I do it, but people do remarkable things every day. Not that what I am doing is remarkable, though it is remarkably soul crushing. I call it a bag because that's what it is. Bags hold stuff. According to the *Australian Modern Oxford Dictionary*, a bag is 'a flexible container with an opening at the top'. Stomal therapists call it a pouch or an appliance. To me, it was just a bag of shit.

Emptying a bag of your own shit into the toilet is one of the most humbling things you can ever do. It can be celebratory or so profoundly harrowing that all you can do is sit on the toilet and cry. The stomal therapist has shown me how to empty the bag, and even though we've done a couple of practice runs, I'm still afraid to go through the process by myself. You secretly hope that the nurses will do it for you forever, but I have to learn how to empty and change the bag.

The first time I do it alone I go to the bathroom sink, fill a jug with warm water and sit on the toilet. Spreading my legs as far apart as I can – but not too far because I don't want to break the skin where a piece of my thigh now sits atop my vulva – I open my gown, look down at the bag, which feels warm to touch. I very deliberately say, 'I can do this' with a simple hope that I can. I unfold and open the bottom of the bag, and the contents not so much pour, but plop into the toilet. I did it. I emptied a bag full of my own shit into the toilet. An all-encompassing sense of relief sweeps through me, and again I speak out loud, this time saying, 'I did it.'

Now all I have to do is pour some warm water into the bag to clean it out. My thoughts turn to when I will have to change the bag, and I'm told that it comes down to personal choice. Some people with colostomies or ileostomies change their bag once a day, while others leave the same bag on for a few days. I plan to change it every two days to reduce the risk of my skin breaking down due to its violent aversion to adhesives, but this is not to be.

When Lizzie and Val come around that afternoon, I tell them I've emptied my bag on my own and receive a small round of applause. Val and Lizzie are not bothered by shit. In fact, they *love* shit. Or more to the point, they love helping people with their shit.

From the pamphlets I've been given, people lead full lives with poo bags. They eat what they want, go out with their friends, swim, play tennis, visit the beach, and take part in other social pursuits. They have sex – good sex – and have careers. I think to myself, *How fucking darling.*

The problems I have in hospital amplify when I go home. The bag leaks, often in several places. Liquid shit runs down my belly and into my groin until it befriends gravity, whereupon it makes a steady stream down my leg, seeping through my clothes. There are explosions of shit when I am supine, and at night I often wake up to a foul stench and feeling wet from the bag exploding clean off my body. There are times when the shit literally hits my ceiling fan, and I wake up with chunks of shit in my hair and on my face. Is this what shit-faced *really* means? When I have my first shower at home, I look down in wonder at the hole in my stomach pumping shit out all over the shower recess. *So, this is my life now*, I think.

Out of everything, the explosions are the hardest to process. In the beginning, it's a shock. I lay in the darkness for as long as I need to gather my thoughts. Then, when I reach for my bedside lamp, the shit rolls clean off my body. After many accidents I get used to it. So much so that whenever it happens, which is at least once a day, I respond robotically and say out loud, 'Shit.' Sometimes I cry or laugh (often both) before the clean-up begins.

I simply can't understand how I've arrived at this juncture in my life. I am thirty, with a broken vagina and a hole in my stomach. Thirty-year-olds don't have poo bags – old people have poo bags.

I soon establish a routine whenever there is an explosion:

Gather thoughts and turn on lamp.

Assess the mess and the size of the clean-up – is there shit on my blanket or is it in situ on my body? Is it in my hair? If so, I can deal with that later.

Slowly get out of bed, ensuring that no shit splatters on the floor.

Walk cautiously to toilet or shower, depending on how big the explosion is.

Sit on toilet and peel off any remaining parts of the bag that are still attached to my skin.

Dump bag of shit into a nappy sack.

Hold a wad of toilet paper over Rosebud in case it decorates the floor or surrounding walls of the toilet with shit (or if there is enough momentum, my chin).

Clean skin around Rosebud with baby wipes, disposing of them in the same nappy sack.

Get out a wafer (no, not one you eat at church), and mould it to size using the heat in my fingers.

Cut a circle in the centre of a fresh bag where it will stick to the wafer and fit it over Rosebud so it can collect shit (don't cut the hole too small or too big).

Wipe the area with a skin prep swab to prevent skin from bleeding and peeling off.

Allow skin to dry.

Attach wafer to skin.

Peel paper off bag to expose adhesive.

Attach bag to wafer and press down using the natural heat of my palms to get a good seal.

Hope to fuck that this is going to be the only explosion tonight/this morning/this hour/today.

Dispose of all other rubbish into nappy sack.

Knot and dispose of nappy sack in the bin.

I would like to publicly thank my mother for hosing down and washing my bedclothes countless times over the three-month shit show.

When I shower, the routine is much the same and, as such, 'Operation Shitstorm' is born. I prepare my supplies and, upon removing the bag, take giant John Cleese–like steps into the shower recess as fast as I can, so if Rosebud is going to erupt, the shit will end up in the shower as opposed to on the bathmat. I become one with Rosebud, despite having the acute desire to be totally separate from it.

During Operation Shitstorm I revel in small achievements like driving my car or walking around the block. It is almost shocking to me that life has gone on. The garbage is collected, the mail still arrives, people go to work, kids go to school. One

Saturday morning, feeling brave, I drive to the West End markets. When I arrive and see the crowds of people, I'm too scared to get out of the car, but I refuse to go home empty-handed. I push on to the Powerhouse Markets at New Farm, where I gingerly climb out of my Jeep and face the public for the first time by myself. I stay for about fifteen minutes because I'm worried my bag will either leak or explode. I walk slowly around the market, buying bread, fruit and fudge, and return home with my bounty, feeling victorious.

⚘

My ileostomy is reversed on 16 January 2008. After the reversal surgery, the warm emanation of my first fart is like welcoming back a long-lost friend.

There is no manual for being in such close company with death, and people expect different emotional responses. I tell Mum that I have an exit plan if my ileostomy reversal isn't successful, and I end up with a permanent colostomy. I know I am not strong enough. I simply do not have the mental tenacity or the desire to live.

'Well, I'm coming with you.'

I worry she isn't joking.

When I wake up post-surgery, the first thing I do is feel my stomach to see if there's still a bag there. I can't feel one – the reversal has been a success, and despite the searing pain, I smile with gratitude and relief. Under nasal prongs, I whisper, 'No bag,' and the nurse looking after me in recovery rubs my shoulder, smiles and says, 'No bag, darling,' and I feel whole again.

I manage to get a nasty and painful infection in my wound, which has to be lanced and drained of pus daily for the next month. It leaves behind an uneven indentation in my gut, and the infection brings me to my knees in the literal sense when Mum has to call paramedics because I can barely breathe with the pain. They load me up with narcotics, and I stay in hospital for a few days because yet again it is proving impossible to get my pain under control. One day, I'm given so much morphine a medical emergency team call is made. I'm given multiple doses of Narcan® – the drug that paramedics use to pull people who have overdosed on heroin back to life.

When I regain consciousness, I am aware something has gone awry from the number of nurses and doctors that flank my bed. I'm just not sure what.

'What happened?' I ask.

'You were having a little trouble with your breathing, love. We're just keeping an eye on you.'

'All ten of you?'

They all nod. I was down to four breaths a minute.

Excellent, I think. *The third time they've nearly killed me in as many months.*

How does one remain tethered to life when it's nearly been ended multiple times? My donor's lungs and I breathe together, yet I did not know her, and I do not know this woman I have become.

⚘

It's a few weeks after I get home that I'm game enough to take my new vulva for a test drive. Despite all I've been through (or *in spite* of it), I need to know if I can still have an orgasm. I feel that a part of my womanhood has been stripped from me – literally and figuratively.

Before my surgery, nearly everything I read about vulva cancer was dire. It's mostly a cancer of elderly women, and I'm the youngest woman in the state – possibly the country – to have undergone such radical surgery. Most women who have radical vulvectomies rarely have fulfilling sex lives again due to pain and other issues. Worse, most never have an orgasm. As a woman who has just turned thirty-one, I worry about not being a fully functioning sexual being.

It doesn't take much coaxing, and when it happens I feel like the sex gods are smiling upon me. I cry, dance around my bedroom and promptly run upstairs to tell Mum.

We high-five and fist-bump in the kitchen, and I talk at length of my relief over a cuppa.

'When you think about it ... I'm basically a born-again virgin.'

After vulva cancer surgery, it is customary to have regular Pap smears and colposcopies – a small procedure to examine your vagina, vulva and cervix. I climb up onto the examination table and hear the sticking sound of the rubber wheels of the metal trolley; the instruments rattling as if in excitement that they're about to be warmed by the walls of my cervix and the inside of my vagina.

The doctor says, 'Bottom as far to the edge of the bed as you can manage.' So, I shuffle as close as I can get without my arse falling to the floor.

'You've done this before,' she says.

I like her. She doesn't say it with an inflection of pity.

'Boots are staying on,' I say.

'As long as I don't cop one in the head, you're more than welcome to leave them on.'

'It's for a dare.'

'Do you get a prize?'

'No. Just the glory.'

'Well next time you'll have to raise the stakes. Make sure you get chocolate or something.'

'I know – I sold myself short. Next time there will be a prize, like a piñata in the shape of a vulva.'

'Ha! I'd love to see that!'

A male medical student looks at my car-crash of a vagina as the speculum is pushed in and screwed into place like a ship in dry dock.

'It still works,' I tell him, raising a smile and a nod.

'That's fantastic,' says the doctor. 'Isn't that great?' she says to the med student.

'Um, yeah – amazing. Really,' he says dispassionately.

Pause.

The nurse hands the doctor the world's biggest Q-tip.

'So, first we're going to paint the vinegar on to see if we can see any abnormal cells, like any vulval intraepithelial neoplasia or any obvious cancer.'

I nod.

'It's going to sting a bit. Apparently, it feels exactly like a cigarette burn.'

'That's a pretty accurate simile.' I look to the medical student. 'If you can imagine, for just a second, a cigarette burn on the tip of your wang.'

'Wow,' he says, stuffing his hands in his pockets and shuffling from foot to foot.

The vinegar is cold; smells acidic. Being a teaching hospital, the doctor talks shop with the med student as he gazes through the colposcope, much like a developer would look at a vacant block of land, determining its topography and worth. That is my vulva. My magical vulva is precious real estate.

Now it's time for more acetic acid, though it feels closer to the consistency of molasses. That done, the Q-tip is given to the nurse who places it back on the trolley to be thrown into the clinical waste bin.

I take photos of my boots, the trolley, the doctor's head between my legs, the sterilised speculums of differing sizes encased in plastic. Taking photos is just something I do – mainly for shits and giggles. Now it's punch biopsy time. Because my last results were abnormal, she needs to send a tissue sample to pathology. A literal cunt punch with a cunt scrape chaser.

'Can I please have some local?' the doctor asks the nurse.

'I don't need local,' I say.

'You sure?'

'A sting is still a sting. Just tell me when.'

'Brave much?'

'I would wager more stupid than brave?'

She positions the punch, says 'when', and a sting radiates through my vulva, up my groin and into my sacrum.

'Well done,' she says.

But it's not over yet. Getting the actual tissue sample out is the painful part. First, the tiny piece of skin that's been nipped by the cunt punch is gripped with forceps and elevated slightly above the skin line. Usually, it will still be connected at the base, so a sterile blade will cut along the bottom, freeing the plug from the subcutaneous tissue.

A stick of silver nitrate is applied to where the biopsy has been taken, which cauterises and seals the skin, stemming any bleeding. The metal dog-trap that's been inside me for twenty minutes is pulled out – a strange feeling of sweet agony. In half an hour, it's over, and the nurse wraps up the dressing pack like a butcher would your weekly meat shop, and casts it into the bin. The room looks as though I've never been there, save for the blood on the edge of the sheet. I pull on my skirt and return to the consulting room, which is where the hard work begins – the head fuck.

What stage is it at?

Has it spread?

What if it's in my lymph nodes?

How much surgery will I need?

Will I have to have another ileostomy?

Will I need chemotherapy or radiation?

I need to know everything. I've always needed to know everything. And then the other questions in the week before I get the all-clear:

Who is going to love me?

Who is going to want me?

In high school, one of my best CF friends was Melinda. We would stockpile Chux cloths from the hospital kitchen, tear them into strips and tie our hair up in 'rags'. We'd take them out the next morning, and for about five minutes our hair cascaded in loose curls down our back. We slathered our faces in green clay masks, styled our hair into pigtails to take photos of each other, and spirited ourselves away into the tiny utilities room or retreated to the abandoned Sylvia Moffatt Ward beneath Adelaide Billing, armed with a boombox, cassettes, snacks and Melinda's nasal prongs so she could stay connected to oxygen. We tried the nitrous oxide, but alas, it had been cut off.

Being the much healthier of the two, I danced while Melinda sat on the floor and laughed until she turned blue. Continuing my performance, I jumped off chairs and climbed on old hospital beds, thrusting my hips until the bed broke beneath me. I scaled old metal cots like a cage dancer, used IV poles for the purposes of pole dancing and 'roller-pole', where I'd squat and try to steer, much like roller derby. Because we were in an abandoned ward, we had plenty of room to move.

The morning after a dance-off, we would wake up with sore necks from head-banging to the heavy metal we loved. No-one knew about our secret junkets downstairs. Once we sealed up the heavy doors of Sylvia Moffatt Ward, we'd jump all over the kitchen's stainless-steel benches, spray syringes of normal saline all over the walls, and, thanks to the concrete and terrazzo between the floors, we would scream knowing no-one could hear us.

In 1992, Melinda met a long, floppy-haired boy called Wayne. Everyone was initially suspicious of his intentions, what with his passion for heavy metal and the T-shirts he wore with gloriously offensive logos. He was a young man of few words, but it wasn't long before everyone realised that he loved Melinda beyond measure. He was one of the most beautiful and devoted young men I had ever met. He was always at the hospital, spending time with Melinda, whether it was taking her out, doing her physio, helping with her antibiotic infusions or just being there.

Our song was 'November Rain', but when Melinda met Wayne it became their song and I happily passed on the torch. I was pleased she had someone else to share it with.

By 1993, Melinda and I had different strains of bugs in our lungs, so we were forcibly separated. In her final weeks, I would sneak into her room to massage her legs; her spine painfully concertinaed from the pressure on her lungs. We talked, and I asked if there was anything I could do, even though I knew I couldn't soothe her pain, which brought the familiar sting of helplessness. I could see she was in an incredible amount of pain, so I rubbed her back when she coughed and rearranged her pillows so they might soften under her spine a little. Because she was effectively drowning, she had to sleep upright.

One day, I snuck into her ward, and I was there not even a minute when we heard the CF liaison nurse in the corridor. Because she had a proclivity for losing her shit at the slightest act of defiance, we started laughing, which meant Melinda started coughing. Hilary would have been livid if she found me, so I made a dash for Melinda's bathroom.

'Fuck,' Melinda rattled, once Hilary had left. 'I never thought ... she'd leave.' She could barely squeeze the words out.

Melinda died in late September, the day after Wayne proposed.

At her funeral, dark skies rumbled with the threat of rain. Her younger sister, who also had CF, was shivering with grief in the front row beside her mother and baby sister. At the end of the service, the first piano strike of 'November Rain' rang out. My head dropped heavily on my chest, and I thought I might throw up. I knew the song would be played, but hearing it meant that this was it. Melinda was gone.

As the song was ending, we gathered outside in the rain. When Slash ripped out his final solo, Wayne turned away from the crowd and began to run. He ran and didn't stop running. He cut a lonely and devastated figure as he sprinted through the cemetery.

I saw Wayne again about six months after Melinda died. He visited me in hospital a couple of times, which I found incredibly courageous. Ballsy, really. To return to the place where he held his great love as she took her final breath was an act of resistance – a big 'fuck you' to CF.

In my early thirties, I began to have night terrors, many of them revolving around Melinda. I began listening to 'November Rain', which is the centrepiece of a trilogy of Guns N' Roses songs from the early 1990s. I listened to it on a loop for hours at a time and watched the accompanying videos, trapping myself in a memory of Melinda's funeral. The videos feature themes of suicide, murder, violence, drowning and death. In a cycle of psychological self-torture, I read my diaries compulsively and looked back over photographs of my dead friends. I realised that each death sharpened the one that came before, each braid of terror fortifying the last.

After Melinda died, I still went down to where we used to dance. The building had been abandoned, and I managed to squeeze through the padlocked doors. You couldn't call it devoid of soul, but it had a distinct paucity of warmth. There was no music, no go-go dancing on counter tops. I sat on the smooth linoleum floor that had been softened and dented with millions of footsteps. And while I might have been alone, I could feel the weight of the thousands of children who had met their end in that awful place.

⚘

After cancer nearly kills me, I am full of fury. I become a handmaiden of anger, and it palpitates through me with a beating thrum of displeasure. So much of my old self had fallen away, and I detested what had unfurled in its place. I was anchored to my past; tethered like a leash. I resisted facing the future.

Instead, I take pleasure in watching videos depicting messy surgeries and looking at gruesome photos, yet I never feel satiated. One day in ICU, as I was about to have a central venous line tunnelled into my jugular vein, I insisted that it be done with the minimum amount of local anaesthetic.

'Why would you want to do that?' I am asked.

'So I can feel the full experience.'

And I do. I feel every stitch being sewn into my skin as though I'm being sutured with hessian twine and a bagging needle. That night I need high doses of fentanyl for the pain.

I derive immense satisfaction in feeling physical pain, and the more committed I am to inflicting pain on myself, the less guilt I feel. Punishing myself is a compulsion I adopt for having survived when so many of my CF friends did not. A constant need to atone for my transplant. I say to myself, 'I deserve it. It's part of my penance. My pain is nothing compared to that of my friends who didn't live.' I hurt myself deliberately as a living testimony to my dead.

My self-harm takes many forms. I abuse drugs and sleep with people I barely know to gain some semblance of control and agency, but mostly because I'm unyielding in my belief that I deserve to suffer. One night, I think it might be novel to cannulate myself. I find a vein in my chest, stand in front of the mirror, palpate the blue streak and pierce my skin. Where I expect to feel a surge of dopamine when I see the flash of crimson in the needle, it's satisfying for all of five seconds. A hollow victory.

It is years before I see that by deliberately subjecting myself to pain, I am digging myself deeper into a trauma cycle. In the years to come, I look back in regret for having locked myself away after the transplant; I should have started living my life from the outset. For me, the transplant becomes a shared responsibility and duty of care with my donor, her family, my medical team and my own family.

In 2007, my best friend Bec is visiting me. Dad's recently bought a bright red E-Type Jaguar, which she hasn't yet seen.

'Come out and have a look. She's beautiful,' I say. 'Actually, you should hear it. You *need* to hear it. I'll grab the keys.'

We walk out to the garage.

'Wow. I can see Rosco in this.'

I hop into the driver's seat, turn the ignition on and scream. There's nothing like the thrum of a V12 engine to make you feel alive.

'Hop in,' I shout above the engine.

After Bec gets in, I throw the car into reverse.

'Carls . . . what are you doing?'

I smile.

'Oh my god, Rosco is going to kill us!'

I laugh, and think, *Rosco isn't here!*

I back the trembling car out of the driveway. I'm used to driving a manual Jeep, but the Jag doesn't have power steering. We take off at great speed, and Bec lets out an almighty scream. I drive around our neighbourhood, then floor it up one of the city's steepest streets only to find the police waiting for us at the top. Bec and I both say, 'Oh, fuck', but all the police do is give us a gentle wave.

'I think that's a sign,' I yell over the heaving engine.

No matter the damage, red-lining the E-Type at ninety kilometres an hour pulls me back into my body. It takes me two years to tell Dad I took his pride and joy for a spin.

He looks at me, and in that moment I think he's going to ground me (even though I'm thirty-three years old).

'Well?'

'Well, what?'

'How'd she go?'

'Like. The. Clappers.'

He lets out a relieved laugh. 'Where was I?'

'Not here.'

'Obviously. Well, I'm glad she ran satisfactorily for you,' he says, returning to his book.

You'd be mistaken if you thought my dad wasn't spiritual. Even though he's only ever attended church for his wedding and the occasional Christmas service, he has an unshakable faith and prays every night. Spirituality has played a looming role in my life from when I was young, and it plays an even bigger role now.

When I first went on the transplant list, my parents' pain at seeing me get sicker and sicker – and being powerless to do anything about it – took its toll. Despite their torment, my dad somehow managed to remain eternally optimistic, offering me financial rewards (bribes) so I'd work harder to increase my lung function.

It wasn't until I'd been on the transplant list for around six months that Dad realised I wasn't going to get better. One day, Ollie brought me to the new house so I could see my room, but I was too sick to get out of the car. In that moment, Dad knew. He knew the day was finally here. CF had come to cash in its chips and claim his daughter. He always knew he might have to deal with my death, but he'd buried these thoughts so deeply in his subconscious that they rarely surfaced. In that moment he knew my odds without a transplant were nil. For my dad, in the face of uncertainty and hopelessness, prayers helped.

I don't have an aversion to being prayed for; if anything, it buoys me because it's a reminder of the kindness of people. When I was on the transplant list one of our close family friends held a prayer circle for me, and I felt such gratitude that it brought me to tears. The word itself comes from Middle English, meaning to 'ask earnestly', which is beautifully secular. It was comforting to know someone was wishing – or asking earnestly – for kindness and goodness for another human being. A well-intentioned prayer is just another form of energy being sent out into the universe; a meditation with a deity attached to it. I might be agnostic, but I still pray. And if someone says to me, 'I'm praying for you', I always give thanks. Prayers can help those doing the praying too.

For a time after my cunt cancer coma, I feel embittered towards religion. But once I devote myself to learning about dying and death, the anger evaporates, and with that comes a wellspring of empathy and radical acceptance. I find that truth serves as a key to unlock knowledge, power and compassion – I'd just done it in reverse order. I did these things after I resurfaced in my new life, where everything had been either forgotten or needed to be relearnt.

⚘

As a teen, I attended an Anglican all-girls school, so prayer was a part of every weekday. In grade eight, I decided to join the order of the Sisters of the Sacred Advent. My divinity teacher was a nineteen-year-old nun called Sister Caroline, and the idea of service seemed to be an extension of my natural skill set. I just wasn't sure about the giving myself to God bit. This phase didn't last long as I soon discovered boys.

Two years after my transplant, I had a crisis of faith, and for six months I pondered joining the Carmelite order of nuns. The Carmelites are a silent order who grow their own food and are self-sufficient. There's a sense of expansion in the silence they keep. I started writing to the head nun at the Carmelites, and we exchanged a few letters, but I realised that I just wanted to live a monastic life minus the religion. Or that is, I wanted a monastic life, but I also wanted sex, wine, swearing and conversation. I was seeking something I wouldn't find until my thirties, and perhaps unsurprisingly, when I did it was service in a spiritual context.

On a spring day in 2009, my friend Lynn, who had nursed me as a teenager, invites me along to a community palliative care centre called Karuna. Karuna is run by Tibetan Buddhist nuns and volunteers, and their stupa is in dire need of tender hands with paint and soft brushes. The stupa is a vital part of Karuna – it's a place where Buddhists come to worship and where anyone can rest to gather their thoughts, meditate, pray, or feel perfect peace.

A few months before, Lynn had undertaken a course called 'Spiritual Care with the Dying', which she told me was a transformative experience for her. I'm lucky enough to nab one of the last spots for the next course, which is to be held as an intensive over five weeks. In a nutshell, it's the most fulfilling and humbling experience of my life.

I walk into Karuna a very frightened woman. Frightened of death after nearly dying under fluorescent lights two years before, and terrified of my parents dying. Over the coming weeks, all twenty-four of us strip our souls bare doing various meditative exercises. The meditation that affects me the most is about three people who are dying – someone we love very much, a stranger, and someone who we have a complicated relationship with. For the stranger, the meditation takes me to a Sikh man who collects the trolleys at my local supermarket. I don't know why I think of him, but I close my eyes, and there he is. I gently unwrap his turban and his hair cascades down his shoulders and onto his chest. I climb into bed where I hold him; hearing and feeling the timbre of his final breaths. He dies with me that day but is resurrected when we exchange smiles the next time I see him at the supermarket, as though we have an unspoken contract of the soul.

I leave Karuna feeling at peace with death and come away with an active practice of loving kindness. It is not so much that my anger melts away as it is completely vaporised.

WHILE THERE IS STILL A part of me that wants to rage, rage, rage, another part of me wants to climb into the quiet of my own heart, much like wading into still water. It takes me a while, but by the time I turn forty, I have managed to curtail my predilection for looking at medical trauma and enter into a trauma-porn remission. My craving for experiencing pain seems to have exhausted itself, although I can see that my past has taken a toll. Was I more resilient when I was younger? Or was I just so busy trying to survive that I didn't have time to step away and reconcile what I'd been through and say, 'Okay, that was intense.' At this juncture of my life, I'm all about the path of least resistance. Going into hospital now is an expedited journey to the seventh circle of hell. If I'm in for longer than one night, I feel like a caged animal.

At the beginning of 2012, I retreat to the Sunshine Coast hinterland to do a ten-day silent meditation retreat, though retreat is a misnomer because a retreat denotes some form of rest and relaxation. Vipassana simply means 'to observe'. There is no speaking, no eye contact, no books, no phones, no writing materials, no music, no jewellery, no essential fucking oils. Nothing. Just pure observation. Nothing to help you not lose your shit.

The morning I leave the city, I get a call from my friend Camille that she's about to go into theatre for a double lung transplant in Melbourne. For the first two days, it's hard to focus because I don't know if she is dead or alive. I have great trouble not being able to say, 'thank you' and 'excuse me' to my fellow students. It feels so rude. On the third day, my teacher, Lee, asks to see me. Most days, each student meets with a teacher to check in. During these sessions we can talk, and Lee tells me Mum has called to let me know that Cam survived the surgery and is stable. I cry with relief and miss the afternoon meditation because my sobbing in the meditation hall would distract the other students. After a rest, I make my way to the hall for that night's meditation and teachings, feeling happy, albeit a little distracted.

The place is a strange kind of magic. Every afternoon, like clockwork, cicadas begin to chirp and the noise pulses through the meditation hall. Of a morning, they sound their song as great skeins of light tumble down across the space behind my eyes. My meditations are bathed in a perpetual shade of yellow.

But it's hard work. A few people leave, some on the second day, others on the fourth. It had been mentioned that the third day is like a reckoning, and while my reckoning arrives, it refuses to leave. Three days in, I'm certain I'm lurching into the depths of madness. It is psychological warfare. Everything plays through my head like a movie in fast motion. Every person I've ever met, every song I've ever heard, every party I've ever been to, every kiss, every sexual experience, every flash of anger, every bereavement, every death, every joy, every pain, every fight, every book I've ever read, every story I've ever written, every movie I've ever seen, every surgery and every medical procedure tears through my head. I have eight days of these non-stop flashes. In the stillness of the meditation hall, I look around and think, 'Everyone's got their shit sorted. Everyone looks so fucking ZEN.' It is a strange comfort knowing that despite appearances, everyone is squaring off with their own demons.

What I come to learn is that the more I crave something (like silence in my head), the further away it gets. We're meditating for ten-plus hours a day, and it's strange what your brain picks up on. At the end of each meditation session, we're played a recording of SN Goenka – the founder of Vipassana – and I notice that about five minutes towards the end, he trills through his nose a word that sounds like an anti-epileptic drug I used to take for migraines.

'Nah, nah, nahhhhh … other highly spiritual shit … TOPIRAMATE.'

The night before I left for the retreat, my friend Lynn said a similar thing had happened to her when, about ten minutes before the end of a session, she'd hear a word and think, 'Thank fuck it's nearly over!'

'Topiramate' worked – the chant, not the drug. The drug sedated me for twenty-two hours a day.

In another meeting with Lee, we talk about the mother lode of guilt I have about my transplant and having outlived most of my friends. The distance between guilt and grief is much like a crack of light through an open door.

'What I'm hearing is that you're very grateful. That's what I'm hearing. I know that's not what you've been feeling, but do you think you could move from that feeling of guilt into gratitude?'

It's like she's dropped a bomb on me, and I move into a space I've never been in before, where for the first time gratitude trumps guilt. It is completely at odds with what I've been feeling for the past fourteen years.

Only once you can stop intrusive thoughts about your past, can you begin fantasising about the future. It took eight days to muddle through the quagmire in my head before I could quieten my mind. When I speak to people afterwards, I realise that this is unique to me.

'On the third day, I was totally at peace.'

Okay.

'Things became really clear on the second day.'

Really.

'Wasn't the hardest thing I've ever done.'

Were you even there?

'I think I'd like to do another one, but for longer.'

JESUS MOTHERFUCK.

'So how did you go?' they ask.

'I was beating the shit out of my head with my water bottle on day eight trying to get the millions of thoughts out of my head.'

'Oh.'

'Thought I was going mad. It was mental. *I* was mental.'

The friends of noble silence are kind and almost as relieved as I am when I eventually stumble into a place of peace.

'You had that shit in your head for eight days?'

Mmmmm.

I resurface clean, ready to push back into the world. I've never felt more calm or centred. My tolerance for other people's intolerance is something I've not felt for many years, and it's as if I can dissociate from certain situations. For example, when I go grocery shopping, I don't hear the beep of the scanners or groaning trolleys. It's as though I'm on another plane. Not separate or better than anyone else, just elsewhere. I even lose my propensity for the only form of aggression I ever get – yelling 'You stupid cunt!' at people who can't drive. Instead, I say, 'Namaste, motherfucker.'

The week after I get home, I find myself in a lavender-coloured gown in the Nuclear Medicine department waiting for a PET scan to rule out metastatic bone cancer. As I'm fed into the machine with my mum looking on, I'm not feeling my usual level of 'scanxiety'. I'm at such a place of peace, I think that if I do have cancer I'll just get on with it. After the scan, I see one of my transplant consultants and the transplant physio.

'I hear you've had some back pain,' says James.

'Yeah, it's been a bit sore. I'm having trouble standing and sleeping. And sitting.'

'Ms Metcalfe, you do not have cancer,' says my transplant consultant, in his clipped German accent.

'Was pretty sure I didn't, but I wanted to make sure.'

'So, you went from not doing any meditation to sitting for ten-plus hours a day on a timber floor?' asks the physio.

I nod.

'Well, that'll do it,' says the physio.

'No more meditation for you,' says Andreas, sounding like the Terminator.

'Don't do things by halves, do you, Metcalfe?' quips James.

'I have no idea what you're talking about.'

⚘

Having plans for my future has always kept me going, kept me sharp. But because I've grown up with the constant threat of death, I am a mess financially. 'I might only have a year to live, so I'll buy those bright blue cowboy boots.' Or, 'I'm on borrowed time with these lungs, so I'll buy that expensive Italian easel.' I never did learn to paint.

I think nothing of frittering my money away because having 'stuff' makes me feel happy. My spending hit fever pitch after my transplant. I was awed that I could go shopping without needing a tank of oxygen for fear of keeling over. I always reasoned that because I had been told I had five years of life left after my transplant, I needed to go bull at a gate with everything. I never expected to live to see my thirties, let alone my forties.

For many years, shopping is an addiction; a temporary salve until I buy the next thing. When I'm abusing drugs, my propensity to spend money is off the charts, and I open my front door to find all sorts of mysterious parcels – things I have no memory of buying. It was difficult enough surviving on a disability pension and there are times when I'm in such dire financial straits it is frightening. I've never owned a credit card, so I never spend what I don't have, but there are weeks when I live on tinned spaghetti after I make such sizeable donations to charity I'm unable to pay my rent.

Looking back, I can see I was suffering from compulsive spending disorder – while I thought I just liked stuff, buying things I don't really need is actually a trauma response. It might sound like a cop-out, but the more I read about compulsive shopping, or oniomania, the more dots I connect.

When I move in 2017, I donate twelve bags of clothing to a charity shop, and I think it quite remarkable what I have managed to accumulate in a small two-bedroom unit. When the young lady behind the counter says, 'That's a lot of clothes', I respond, 'It's a disgrace'. I walk out feeling both ashamed and considerably lighter. I don't blame consumerism or capitalism. This was on me, and it was up to me to disentangle myself. These days, I shop out of necessity. I stay away from shopping centres; not because they're tempting, but because they make me feel claustrophobic. I do my best to eschew fast fashion and I'm an avid recycler. In high school I had a passion for op-shopping, mostly because I didn't have the financial means to shop anywhere else, and the things I liked – velvet dresses, tulle skirts, Doc Marten boots, anything tie-dyed, essential oils and crystals – are impossible to source in retail shops. The adage is true – old hippies never die.

TEN MONTHS AFTER THE RETREAT, I'm back in the arms of Morpheus. What started out as taking OxyContin as a migraineur circles back into dependence fuelled by the guilt I feel at being alive. As always, I've hidden it well from everyone. The only problem is that there's only so long you can hide something like a raging narcotic addiction from yourself. Addiction leaves you bereft of space in your head and your soul, and I found myself with one foot planted in this world and the other in the next – again.

At its core, addiction is a well of loneliness, amoral choices and an excess of sleep. I've always been a night owl and a big sleeper, but when I'm using drugs, I'm positively crepuscular. I sit at my desk and try to write – a place where so many marvellous ideas come to rot on the vine. I fall asleep with my finger on the keyboard, and the next day I have to delete pages of the letter my hand had fallen on. Around one o'clock in the morning, I wake up, brush my teeth, swallow some benzos and drop into bed. I won't wake until ten – at the earliest – in the morning.

Apart from when I go out for gatherings with family and friends (many of which I miss), I spend months in darkness, my life unspooling before me. I fall over and open cupboards into my head. I sprain ankles, and am fairly sure I fractured a rib after a fall. There was no need for a visit to hospital because I already had the painkillers. One night, I take so much OxyContin, my heart launches into a series of arrhythmias. Instead of calling an ambulance, I lie on the floor of my bedroom giving myself chest compressions. I do this for twenty minutes and wonder if this is the moment my heart falls into a rhythm where it stops and my body is discovered the next day by my building super, Alex. Would he be okay? He used to be a cop and had told me stories about picking up decapitated heads from the side of the road. I catastrophise about my parents having police arrive at the family home to deliver a death message, and then mull over how comical it would be if I died from a drug overdose after having survived the unsurvivable. As I tamp down on my chest with the heel of my hand, I ask myself, 'Would I really be such a great loss when I'm such a burden? Maybe it would be a relief for everyone if it ended now. If *I* ended. Tonight.'

The next day I get high again.

In September 2013, I fly out to Barcaldine – a town in remote western Queensland – to see the family of an old CF friend. I grew up with Meagan, who died about nine months after my transplant. I'm six days into a two-and-a-half-week stay when I realise I have a problem. I'm fast running out of the OxyContin I've been living on for months and am forced to ration what pills I have left.

Fidgeting, pacing and shifting my weight from foot to foot is bearable when I'm moving around, but as soon as I lie down, my legs kick into the air like I'm a marionette and someone is pulling the strings with inhuman force. Each night, under an inky sky with its bursting mantle of stars, my legs piston into the air from akathisia; I squirm like a colicky baby, move my body back and forth and side to side, and pace the floor.

On the afternoon I finally fly home, I call Mum.

'I'm addicted again,' I weep into the phone. In the lentil aisle of Coles, she couldn't be more supportive or loving and reassures me we will get through this together.

Once I resolve to get clean, I am ripped back to all of the times I've gone cold turkey. I'm terrified of going through the brutal physical withdrawal and worried I'll be put on methadone – something so many people never come off. I make an appointment to see my GP, and she tells me about Suboxone, an opioid antagonist that blocks both symptoms of withdrawal and the euphoria that comes with taking opioids. She calls a medical practice that specialises in addiction science. Her first concern when asking for a specialist is, 'But is he nice? Like, really, *really* nice? Because my patient is really, *really* lovely.'

I move home for the interim at the behest of my parents and stay longer than I plan to – not because I have to, but because I want to. Staying at Mum and Dad's acts as a circuit breaker, and I need to be around my family while I readjust to my drug-free reality. The second I make the decision to get clean, I know I'll never use again, but I have completely blown my parents' trust and need to rebuild my relationship with Dad. Mum is more sympathetic because she has carried me through everything, essentially nursing me for my first twenty-one years. When I was on the transplant list, I aged backwards. I needed help with the most rudimentary tasks, like bathing and dressing. She had walked with me through the other seasons of my addiction, whereas Dad hadn't been born with the same insouciance as Mum.

I'm given enough OxyContin to tide me over until I see my addiction specialist. I'll call him The Shaman. Mum and I are immediately smitten. He explains how the process works, doesn't treat me like I'm 'less than', and puts me at ease when he confirms I won't go into physical withdrawal. On that first day, he asks me an unexpected question.

'Why do you think you started taking drugs again?' he asks.

I think about this and begin to cry.

'There must be a part of me that's unhappy. I think I'm just really, really sad.'

Mum cries too.

We leave his rooms and walk into the heaving locus of the hospital, where I'm given my first dose of Suboxone at the pharmacy – a green and bitter, lime-tasting sliver of film I place under my tongue. I'm given a few to take home, but after that, I go to my local chemist every week and line up at the junkie counter to get my weeks' worth of Suboxone. In time, it becomes every two weeks, but that is as far as we can legally stretch it. I despair every time I go to the junkie counter to be dosed but leave feeling humbled. There are addicts in every conceivable shape, and I'm well aware how fortunate I am to have a home, a loving family and friends, and more than adequate medical support. The repartee I have with my chemist is the only thing I miss when I taper off the Suboxone two years later. Being clean releases me into a world where colour, sound, taste and smell slowly return. I come to understand that my life is one of constant reawakenings.

I don't have much to show from my days of addiction, except for a lot of books. Physically, I'm lucky to have escaped unscathed with my liver, kidneys and heart in pristine condition. What isn't immediately clear is the damage I've done to my brain; it's an exercise in futility trying to retain information the way I once could.

Not long after I start opioid antagonist therapy, I enrol in a Master's degree in Spiritual Care and struggle with what my brain is asking of me. After six months, I defer, then withdraw from the course altogether. Throughout the subsequent years, my brain has healed itself thanks to the wonder of neuroplasticity, and while I didn't replace one addiction with another, sometimes I wish I had with exercise and centrifugal juicing.

As an adjuvant therapy, The Shaman recommends seeing a psychologist who integrates meditation and Eastern philosophy into their practice. I make an appointment, and the following week, at our first session, The Therapist does something that no-one has ever done – he takes a complete family history, which morphs into a trauma history. He's curious to know how I've arrived at this point, crawling with a drug habit that wasn't far from killing me. He gently takes me back through time to both my parents' and grandparents' upbringings. The more detail, the clearer the picture.

On a giant whiteboard stuck to his office wall, I watch as a marker jumps up and down. After about half an hour, my life is laid out before me in a scribble of black. I notice that it's complicated. I also notice that The Therapist has had to stop writing because he's out of room. I make another appointment.

Over time, The Therapist gently cracks open a space for me that no-one else ever has; he is a human cushion of compassion, offering me a soft place to land.

'What do you think is wrong with me?' I ask point blank.

The Therapist gives one of his knowing smiles. 'Well, there's nothing wrong with you. Actually, for what you've been through, you're extremely well adjusted. More well adjusted than most people who have been through a lot less.'

'I don't feel like I have an addictive personality.'

'I don't think you have an addictive personality. What I do think is that you really like narcotics and the way they made you feel. Is that something you would ever talk about with me?'

Oof.

Trauma-related addiction is well documented, and while I've never had an eating disorder or suffered from phobias or compulsive sexual behaviours (ravenous libido aside), my fondness for narcotics and barbiturates is more than enough to fuel addiction. I never take them again. At least, I never take them to block my emotional pain, and when I do need them for genuine pain, they make me sick. I throw up, my skin goes clammy, and I itch and panic. Where they once brought me peace, all they bring now is dread.

In August 2014, my oldest CF friend, Sean, is dying of rejection. We had our transplants just two weeks apart; a few years later, Sean had a single lung transplant. Chronic and acute rejection has been his foe, and it has come to claim him. A couple of weeks before I fly down to see him, we're chatting on the phone. He says that after all the friends we've lost, despite being an avowed atheist he wants a sign to prove otherwise.

'You know, just one person to come back, or a sign, so I know that there's more to this. One fucking person, just so I know they're there,' he says.

Like the most secular of people, it's not uncommon to feel comforted there is *something*, just not nothing. I tell him we are never truly alone, but he isn't sold. I fly down to Melbourne to see him. My friend Camille picks me up from the airport, and by the time we get back to her place, it's late. I call Sean's sister, Shannon. She asks if I can get to the hospice as soon as possible. Sean is fading fast and isn't expected to see the night through after having been put on a morphine pump earlier that day. We have about a forty-minute drive ahead of us, but it's a Sunday so traffic is light. I do not want Sean to leave me without getting to say goodbye.

You'd better not die on me, I keep saying in my head. *Don't you fucking dare.*

When we reach the hospice there are a few close friends and family in the waiting area, and Shannon stops short of pushing me into the room, telling me to spend as long as I need with her brother. I walk into the darkened room. The cadence of his breath is uneven and rattly, his mouth open. This is not unusual for Sean. I lean over his bed and stroke his hair and say quietly, 'Hey Seany. It's Carls. I'm here. I made it.'

I say his name a few times, sweep the hair from his clammy forehead. Then the last thing I am expecting happens: he comes to.

He breathes out my name.

'I'm here, honey. I love you.'

And then he begins to speak. We cover politics; he comments with barely any life left in him that the entire front bench are as useless as tits on a bull, with which I agree. Then, holding my hand he says, 'Everyone's here. Everyone's here and they're all looking at you.' Our friends had come through and Sean had his sign, and what a crowded sign it was. I look up and whisper, 'Hi' to acknowledge our friends who are surrounding us. I *feel* them there. The air is buzzing with an energy I've only experienced a few times in my life, and I silently thank them for ferrying Sean on his way.

Shannon and a couple of friends come in, and we have a Baileys. Sean wants a Baileys coffee, so I gently place a palm behind his head and encircle the other around the cup, which he swiftly brushes away, determined to drink it himself. *His* way. And here is when I understood why. Here is a man – a proud man, a fiercely intelligent, witty man – who wants to die with dignity. And to die with speed. I spend some more time with him, get the nurse to give him more pain relief. He tells me he's happy, and I say that I'll see him in the morning. Our last words are, 'I love you.'

I don't sleep. My head might feel heavier than a medicine ball, but I am still in the room with my friend – all of our friends. My body buzzes and pings with energy, and I see sparks firing off my skin in the dark.

⚘

When I arrive at the hospice the next morning, Sean is sitting up in bed, fully cognisant (think intelligent, rude, witty) and eating. He has not long ceased taking all of his transplant medication and isn't having any artificial feeding so he can control his dying process and make it as short as possible. I begin to wonder how long it's going to take if he's eating again and therefore fuelling his body. When you've grown up surrounded by dying, you tend to ponder things like this. He eats his entire lunch; even closely inspecting the viscosity of the pumpkin soup. Knowing the trajectory of a CF death, I can see Sean needs more morphine and a relaxant to make him comfortable. The nurses agree. By the time I leave later that afternoon, he's well sedated.

Not long after lunch, we're introduced to a lovely lady who is taking photos for the hospice. Sean's brother-in-law takes a photo of Sean and me snuggling in Sean's bed as he cracks dirty jokes and grabs my arse.

'You're quite a peach. Remind me why we never slept together?' Sean asks.

'I am quite a bit younger than you. I don't think it would have gone down well,' I say.

'But I go down well.'

'I've no doubt, darling.'

'Ha.'

'Well, you fucked every other CF girl.'

'Only a few. Only the best.'

'You're such a slut.'

I see him one more time, but by this stage he's deep in the

arms of a CF coma. It surprises and upsets me that it takes him so long to die, but what doesn't upset or surprise me is that he wanted to die alone. He didn't want anyone present for his last breaths. True to form, Sean was in full control.

I am (happily) tasked with being the funeral celebrant at his Brisbane memorial later that month.

Shannon would later give me a bottle of his ashes and he sits in my bathroom for a few years. These days, he's in my bedroom. A view I know he would appreciate.

Later that year, I'm invited to speak at TEDx Brisbane. Being asked to speak about my life feels like a defining moment. I have three weeks to prepare my talk. I reflect on a conversation I had long ago with an acupuncturist who was a doctor based in Oxford Street at the height of the AIDS epidemic. We were talking about how many CF friends I'd lost, and he shared his own experience of collective and cumulative grief from losing hundreds of people in his community. I realise that around the same time, we were both seeing our friends die – him as a young GP in Sydney and me as a young kid.

'How did you cope?' I asked him.

'Probably the same way you did. You just do,' he said, flicking another needle into my neck.

To love and be loved is like facing both sides of the moon. It is joy and it is pain. The only thing that got me through so much loss was having others by my side. My survival has never been purely a solo effort. For me, the personal has always been universal. I write my whole talk in less than an hour. I make some edits and send it to my producer. He calls me unexpectedly.

'Your talk,' he says, 'I just don't think it's going to gel with the audience. I don't think they're going to get it.'

At my core, I am an ocean of calm, and it takes a lot for me to lose my shit. After revisiting some awful memories, I take a deep breath and ready myself to bite my tongue. But instead, I blurt out, 'You have no idea how hard it's been looking at photos of dead kids. How dare you tell me to A, change my talk and B, suggest that the audience is stupid!'

I hang up in tears and call my friend Stephen, who has read my speech.

'What a cunt. Don't change a fucking word.'

'I won't.'

'Carls,' he says sternly.

'Yes?'

'He's a fuck-knuckle. Promise me you won't censor yourself.'

'I promise.'

I get a similar response in a message from The Shaman. 'It is brutally honest, full of humour and life,' he writes. 'To me, it was more about life than death. I am sorry that I cannot be there for the real thing.'

As it turns out, my talk 'gels' just fine, and as soon as I wind up my speech, the producer bounds onto the stage and throws his arms around me, in tears, telling me how brilliant I am. I feel euphoric, but I'm still thinking about how irascible he'd been in that phone call. At drinks that evening we start talking, and it's abundantly clear what's going on. He's a man in his mid-fifties who has young children.

'You're terrified of death, aren't you?'

'Um, yes.'

'It's because you've got kids, isn't it?'

'How did you know?'

Over a glass of wine, we talk about dying, death and legacy, and I leave later that evening thinking that if I had influenced just one person to have a conversation about dying and death, my work here was done.

In my twenties, I worried that I was a heartless bitch, and I deduced that this was why bad things kept happening to me and the people I loved. I struggled to empathise with certain people. It wasn't the way I was built – it was more about who I'd become. If a friend's grandparent died, I acknowledged that this was an immense loss, but my inner voice would whisper, *They had a good innings.* This was perhaps a defence mechanism of sorts. Now, I sit with the sadness. Even so-called 'expected deaths' are devastating. We are rarely ever ready for someone we love to die, even when their suffering is protracted and when the only mercy is for it to end.

I've never been good at crying. For most of my life, it has pained me to cry in front of other people because it makes me feel inferior, weak. It tends to bruise my pride because I am Carly, and more than anything, I am strong. At least this was what people told me.

I talk about my inability to cry with The Therapist.

'I know that it was as a kid, after I was a patient in CFTU, that I began to take the less is more approach.'

'What's CFTU?'

'The child and family therapy unit. It was the ward for mad kids. When you're in a place like that, you learn to shut your mouth. We didn't call it the child and family torture unit for nothing.'

I tell him about the time I was admitted to the CFTU because I wasn't being compliant with my treatment. I don't think any child would be happy about being beaten on the chest and back for an hour every day. I'd wriggle around like a worm and try to get out of physio any way I could – whether that be by subterfuge or bad behaviour. Mum and Dad were exhausted from trying to literally pin me down. I remember there being family meetings with a psychiatrist who had an unfortunate pairing of coke-bottle-thick glasses and a beard that was more akin to pubic hair. In one session, he kept emphasising the word 'hate'. He repeatedly asked my mother how much she must hate doing physio every day, how much she must hate giving me my tablets and dealing with my non-compliance. Mum remembers trying to make the point that hate had nothing to do with what was going on, but this didn't match the doctor's narrative. Instead, he tried to elicit fear and failure from my parents, their discussion lasting for over an hour as Mum attempted to wrangle him away from the concept of hate.

I unfold the story about the kids in the CFTU with major mental health issues like depression, anorexia, suicidal ideation and gender dysphoria. There was a stigma about these kids, even at that tender age. I know that no-one and nothing will ever be able to piece them back together – not therapy, not force-feeding, not bullying, not pulling privileges or offering false promises. At mealtimes, we would all eat together in the dining room. The anorexics scream and writhe around on plastic chairs as they're force-fed. If they vomit, they're force-fed again. It occurs to me that parents are given as little information as possible, and should we dare speak out, they are told that we are being manipulative to avoid the responsibility of our illness. I'm only allowed to see my parents every second day for an hour, and any sense of safety disappears when they leave. Days are spent talking to counsellors, time alone in my room, and doing redundant activities like art therapy, which was one step removed from a Rorschach.

Every night when I shower with the other girls, we're watched by a coterie of male nurses. We're not allowed to lock the shower door in case we try to either hang or drown ourselves, so the door is left wide open. Even for a ten-year-old, this stands out to me as being very odd. The 'rules' prohibit us from using the locks, so why they even put them on baffles me until I work out that nurses could – and did – lock insubordinate patients in the cubicles; the locks can be opened and closed from the outside.

This provokes a feeling of fear, and it is the first time I feel violated. Two male nurses, in particular, like to watch us shower. They sit back in their chairs and look at us as if they're at a peep show. While I know what they're doing is wrong, even if at that age I couldn't necessarily articulate why, when you're trying to get out of a psychiatric facility you are nothing but one hundred per cent compliant. You never question. You always listen. You shut your mouth.

'So, you learnt that you needed to keep quiet. Do you think maybe there is a similar reason why you have this aversion to crying?'

'Well, it's just occurred to me that maybe someone said something to me when I was really young. Something about how crying was either wrong or weak. It had to have been a doctor because it wasn't my parents.'

'That would make sense. I mean, your parents were always really free about you showing emotion, weren't they?'

'They were, but I can't remember a time when I didn't feel pathetic for crying.'

I'm well into my thirties before telling my mother how I was eyeballed and how it created an underbelly of menace. Understandably, she is livid.

'Why didn't you tell me earlier?'

'We had more pressing things to deal with. And besides, Dad would've put several people into intensive care, and they wouldn't have been worth the jail time.'

I tell my father and he responds exactly as I predicted.

'Why didn't you tell me? I would've bloody sorted it. Jesus, if I'd known …' he says, drumming his fingers on the kitchen table.

'I know. You would have broken their legs.'

'I would've done more than that.'

I can't fault his desire to keep myself and my sister safe.

A week or so before I'm admitted to the CFTU, Dad's older brother, Garth, has a massive heart attack during an angiogram. I honestly don't believe he will die because in my world only the very young died. Death didn't happen to people Uncle Garth's age. My dad takes me to ICU to visit Garth, where he's on life support. He occasionally responds to having his hand squeezed, but these are dashed hopes.

I now realise that the shrinks got to my parents when they were at their most vulnerable. What an impossible time for them, having to leave me in a strange place down at the bottom of the hospital, then crossing the river to see Garth in ICU every day. I often think about how this would have also affected my sister. Understandably, she's blocked a lot from her memory, but she once wrote in a message:

> *I remember when we went up to the hospital and they wouldn't let us in to see him. I remember being devastated about that. Not long after, I was shopping at Indooroopilly when my name was called over the PA system. I had to go and meet Mum at the information desk, and that's when she told me Garth had died. Then I remember driving to his funeral in the Statesman*

and seeing Dad cry for the first time. Mum was holding his hand while he was driving. I hated seeing that.

The day my uncle dies is the day I'm liberated from the CFTU. I'm downstairs in the activities room, painting a plaster cast of Donald Duck when my father walks in. He's bleary-eyed and, in that moment, I know that my uncle is dead. I stop what I'm doing as he walks over to the table, crouches down and cries as he tells me that Garth has died. I grab on to him with my arms as we bawl our eyes out together. He picks me up, and we walk outside to the car. A nurse runs after us.

'When will you have Carly back?'

That was the wrong question to ask him.

'She's never coming back to this fucking place.'

Dad was never one to mince words, but I'd never heard him say 'fuck' before. It impresses into me that swearing means business.

We tear out of the tiny car park, and I never see another mental health doctor again. The next phase of sadness has come. My dad's beloved brother – the kindest man in the world – has died so arbitrarily and, as we would later find out, his death had been entirely avoidable. It's the first time since the death of my maternal grandfather that I remember that older people *do* die. I'd been conditioned to believe it only happened to kids, so Garth's death doesn't yet feel real.

When I get home, I feel as though I've failed my parents because the CFTU is a place where only the truly broken and fucked up kids go. It's the only time I can remember feeling ashamed. What if the kids at school find out I'd been in a psych ward? What must the nurses in my CF ward be thinking? Would they treat me differently? Had I failed them? Now I've come to see that the only thing that failed was the medical system itself.

I tell The Therapist about the doctor who yelled at me that I needed to grow up and take responsibility for my illness.

'He what?'

'Yeah.'

'And you were eight?'

'Yeah. I know he wouldn't have been the only one who got mad at me, but he's the one I remember.'

'So, he yelled at you for just being a child, and for his own failings, you mean?'

The Therapist walks me through a meditation, and ushers me back in time to my childhood, and after I come back into the room, he asks how I feel, if there's anything that's popped up.

'Could it be *that* doctor?'

'Maybe. I've always felt like a weak piece of shit when I cry, even at funerals. I hold my breath to stop the tears even when I'm on my own. I feel like there's a camera on me, and the world is looking at me and laughing – a bit like *The Truman Show*.'

It's also true that I do most of my crying alone because I fear upsetting other people – especially my parents. As a recovering people pleaser, I still do most of my crying in private, but I can now cry in the pasta aisle of a supermarket without feeling self-conscious. I don't flush with shame like I once did.

At the end of 2020, I make an emergency appointment to see The Therapist.

'There's something *really* wrong,' I tell him. 'I think I've lost all of my compassion. I am a horrible person – a really horrible person.'

'Why do you think that?'

'I just don't care about things like I used to.'

'Maybe you've cared too much in the past and this is just you equalising.'

The man is worth his weight in gold, but I'm not convinced.

'I can't cry.'

'Can you cry at all?'

'Only when I see videos of animals in pain or think about my dog dying. I don't even cry when it comes to other people or even when I think about my dead friends.'

'Which of course brings another layer of guilt for you, yes?'

The man gets me.

Over the course of an hour, The Therapist deduces that I'm not the heartless bitch I think myself to be.

'I just worry that my compassion has reached its end.'

'If you take into account the pandemic – as well as all of the other stuff you've had going on – you've essentially had your life threatened for the millionth time,' he says.

He's right. When the pandemic first reaches our shores, I have to isolate for four months. Not a soul enters my house, and I don't leave. The only time I go out is when I pick up my new puppy, Billie, and take her for her vaccinations, and even then I have to hand her over because humans aren't allowed in the vet surgery.

'That's no small thing,' he says, 'and it's amplified for you because your chances of survival aren't great.'

He's right again. For the first eighteen months of the pandemic, my only treatment option was to be put in an induced coma and placed on life support. This petrified me because I had seen too many friends put on ventilators only for them to die. Even after developing treatments that are more effective than being placed on life support, my transplant consultant says my chances of survival are around 15 per cent should I get Covid. Not great odds.

'I think you've had so much going on, I'm surprised that you're as upbeat as you are.'

'So, I'm not a cold-hearted bitch?'

He smiles. 'You've never been a cold-hearted bitch, Carly.'

My concern is that my wellspring of empathy has run dry, but science tells us that stress and uncertainty impacts our capacity for empathy. It's about self-preservation. Science also tells us that when our lives are at risk, we become hypervigilant, which is our body checking in to see if we're okay. Our primitive system is engaged to help us survive, and we either fight, fly or freeze. When it gets down to it, it's an issue of safety. So, while I fret about having turned into an uncompassionate bitch, there's an explanation. From an evolutionary standpoint, as a species we wouldn't have survived had we not been a little selfish.

And yet, I still can't shake the feeling that I'm not as kind as I once was.

A couple of months later, my friend Brandon is dying from antibody rejection – a rare type of rejection that can happen with organ transplants. I contemplate calling The Therapist again after writing the following in my diary:

> *Brandon gets ever closer to the end, and I feel nothing. Not especially sad – just uncomfortably numb. It makes me feel an immense sense of guilt that I'm not feeling anything. I'm not even feeling the level of guilt I'm used to feeling. I've been reading about emotional numbness and trauma, and this is probably why I'm not feeling anything. I can laugh and feel pangs of joy, but it's as if my other emotions have washed away.*

But instead of reaching out to The Therapist, I decide to sit with the feeling. Brandon dies a day later and the only thing I feel is relief.

On a gusty day in 2017, I say a tentative goodbye to my second home, the Royal Children's Hospital. I pull up, get out of my car and watch the buildings being torn asunder, seemingly eaten by strange-looking machines with metal spikes for teeth. A sickening feeling washes over me as if I've abandoned my friends and I want to run into the dusty fray to what? Save them?

I'm standing on the other side of the road, and it feels like we've been split in half – I am here, they are there. I haven't been into the bowels of the children's hospital for twenty-four years, but I can see the bones of my childhood being picked apart. It was the place where I fell in love for the first time. So many firsts and lasts. So many endings. Too many endings.

I cry as I stand on the side of the road in front of confused workmen. They are kind and walk over to see if I'm okay. I tell them that it had been my second home, and an old guy who's propping up a sign looks at me as if he gets it.

'You're going to be okay.'

'How do you know?'

'You've come this far.'

I reach my mid-thirties before I can drive past it without crying, and I have to drive past it a lot.

In August 2018, Mum and I return to the old children's

hospital campus for a goodbye that is both strange and tender. It's a cloudless and crisp winter day. Most of the old hospital I grew up with is long gone, the last remaining vestiges demolished. While there's a lilting sense of grief, there is also a sense of affection. I feel a shift. Nothing seismic, but it's something I haven't felt before – the sense of an ending.

I share stories with the two lovely ladies who have serendipitously organised this visit on a Royal Exhibition Show public holiday. Where there would normally be the clamour of machines and a mantle of dust, we're met with a cavernous silence. A chaplain I know is also there, and Mum and I regale everyone with stories of utter sacrilege and mischief.

As the winter sun beats down on our shoulders, I say a prayer, throw a tumbled rose quartz into the hole where my life had once been, and feel myself leave my body. I pray for my friends and all the children who died on that hill, and for the next twenty-four hours, I feel suspended above my body as it pings with energy.

⚘

That same year, I get serious about writing this book. I spend many hours reading about trauma – that tense epicentre of human experience. I have a thousand questions no-one can give me answers to. There's an abundance of research on kids with cancer, adults with cancer, multiple sclerosis (MS), and a whole raft of other illnesses, but research about children growing into adulthood with CF – as well as the concept of survivorship – is barely extant. There are a few first-person accounts, but none resemble my own experience of dying and death during childhood. I take the adverse childhood trauma (ACT) test, and there's not one box I can tick. It leaves me feeling confused and like a failure. I pin too much hope on it to give me some answers, but none of the questions or experiences applies to me. Mercifully, I've never been sexually abused. I've never been neglected or experienced domestic violence; my parents have never been to prison or had substance abuse problems. On the surface, my life has been the inverse of the childhood trauma test. I've been loved, supported, cared for, and my family life has been stable.

A friend who is no longer a friend once said to me, 'Your stuff isn't like … you know … it's not as if you were raped. Your treatments have always been consensual. You always knew what you were getting into.' I felt a distinct coil of unease and didn't have the mental clarity to tell her that I didn't consent to being born with CF or the brutal treatments I was subjected to as a child.

When I think about my childhood and adolescence, I feel extraordinarily lucky. My mind wends its way back to think about the CF kids who had the world against them – those who went unloved, kids who lived in squalor with no sense of safety or stability, kids who were sexually abused (I knew of a few), kids who had to deal with domestic violence and kids whose parents would leave them in hospital when they needed some 'me time'. When I ruminate on my own childhood and adolescence, I can see that I got off relatively unscathed. So why do I find it maddening that I scored zero on a test I found on the internet?

In the blustery confines of winter, I come close to losing my mind, activating my nervous system to breaking point. Writing my stories down feels like a brutal act – so far away from the healing and empowering experience I've heard other writers talk about. I've always been proactive when it comes to my mental health because my life has been punctuated with severe depressive episodes, so I make an appointment to see a psychiatrist.

Sitting in her rooms feels like home, with striking South American embroideries on the walls and a warm Persian rug to rest my feet on. She air kisses her patients when they walk through the door, her hair is a mass of curls, and her fashion sense is devastating in that it makes me feel very beige.

'What brings you here today?' she asks.

'I'm not doing very well. At least, I don't think I am.'

We go through my symptoms: extreme lethargy, no motivation, feeling an endless sense of sadness and regret, the sense of being underwater.

'What's different?'

'I've been writing my memoir,' I say.

'I see,' she says, lowering her glasses. 'And what's that been like?'

'Harder than I thought. I knew it wouldn't be cathartic, but I wasn't expecting this.'

We speak about the lack of catharsis.

'It hasn't been liberating or empowering. It's been awful. Really, it's been fucked.'

We speak about my having an almost photographic memory and how it seems that the older I get, the more I remember.

What Doctor H says next stuns me. 'I can't say that I've ever met anyone like you.'

'In what sense?' I figure she's been practising for upwards of forty years, so she's treated thousands of patients with complex trauma.

'You've had most of your friends die of CF, and the best comparison I can come up with – and this is just off the top of my head – is that you're like a survivor of the Holocaust.'

And then I see it. Me, alive, with a litany of dead trailing behind me.

'Carly, you're an outlier. And outliers are a rarity in this world. You've survived the unsurvivable.'

I nod and realise that being a lantern bearer for the dead has become too heavy for me. All I can think on the train ride home is, 'Holocaust, Holocaust, Holocaust' and how utterly abnormal it is. Also, that I'm in a largely empty train carriage, which is several shades of ironic.

At our next appointment, I'm armed with research I've done about norepinephrine-dopamine reuptake inhibitors, which work on dopamine receptors as opposed to selective serotonin reuptake inhibitors (SSRI) that work on our serotonin receptors. The doctor knows I've been on nearly every SSRI type of antidepressant, and I'm running out of treatment options. I'm worried I will never come out of this; that I'll be stuck in a perpetual cycle of subterranean black until I die.

'What do you know about this as an antidepressant?' I ask.

'I know it can be very effective, but it's not used as much over here as it is in America.'

We decide to roll the dice because I have nothing to lose. It's a drug mainly used for people trying to quit smoking and the irony is not lost on me. The drug saves my life.

Over the years I have amassed a small library of books on childhood trauma, and not many resonate. In fact, they leave me with a sense of being even further away from myself. As it turns out, I had been reading all the wrong books.

I'd always been generous with sharing my story but became a rabid over-sharer after mistakenly believing that the more I shared, the more people would understand me and that might help me forge a path to my own understanding. That's not to say all of my over-sharing was harmful. Sometimes it was helpful when I was bonding with others over a painful past, but this could morph into a toxic trauma bond and attracted people who wanted to use me as their own private psychologist. For most of my life, I've been a rescuer, a fixer. 'My name is Carly, and I can and will solve your problems.' In my early thirties, I would spend half the day on Facebook being people's personal therapist. I didn't necessarily invite people to share their problems, but sometimes damaged people both subconsciously and purposefully seek out other damaged souls. I'd find myself awake at 2.00 am helping someone I barely knew who lived on the other side of the world. Facebook was the perfect conduit for over-sharing (and over-helping), but I curbed this predilection, deleted my account, and retreated. What I wouldn't find out until years later is that over-sharing is a trauma response.

I also realise that I fear leaning too hard on people. I don't do 'asking for help' very well, and this is, perhaps, a response to having been looked after my whole life.

⚘

At one point in my thirties, I find myself in a 'situationship'. I know this person is not for me when I get sick and he says, 'I can't imagine being in a relationship with someone who gets sick.'

Oh.

Like a ricochet, I immediately think: *If I loved you, I could totally handle it if you were in a car crash and could never walk again. I would look after you, take you all the way through rehab and bring you home, where we would start our new life together – no matter how hard it would be.* Not that I say this – he doesn't deserve to hear even the seed of that thought.

One Saturday, he calls around midnight saying he's been in a fight. He's only down the road, so I tell him to come to my place. I clean the blood off him, and we go to bed. Not being used to sharing my bed, I can't get to sleep, but he is unconscious.

I begin to hear what sounds like a trickle.

Then the trickle turns into a gush. My situationship is pissing my bed. I run to get some towels, and he is so drunk that I can't wake him up. The peeing won't stop. There is so much pee. At the time, I have a CV line in my jugular for IV antibiotics to treat a lung infection, and while he helps me move the mattress out onto my balcony the next morning, he's long gone by the time it needs to be brought back in. After I wrangle it inside (and it nearly falls seven storeys to its piss-soaked death), I feel a trickle of my own snaking a path down my neck. I touch my neck and when I pull my fingers away they're covered in blood. Because the mattress is so heavy, I've nearly popped the stitches that are holding the line in my jugular. I know I'll be fine because the line is sewn into my skin, but I consider how clichéd it would be if I exsanguinated after being pissed on. Piss, blood, death.

Later that morning, I go to brunch with a friend. While I think it's quite unsavoury that this person has peed in my bed, I'm mostly nonplussed. But Nicole is raging.

'Carls! He pissed in your bed!'

'Yeah,' I said, sipping my French Earl Grey.

'That's really fucked up. You could have died trying to get your mattress back inside.'

'I know.'

'Starting right now I'm going to teach you about boundaries.'

She tells me that it's beyond reproach that this person had me playing Florence Nightingale while I was fighting a nasty lung infection. It is in this moment over delicate ribbon sandwiches that I begin to learn about boundaries. It takes me a while to get 'boundaried', and as someone who avoids conflict (unless it's with doctors), it's an ongoing process. My friend Keri says, 'Having boundaries isn't about creating fierce walls and barricades. Boundaries are about being in the right relationship with yourself and therefore everything and everyone else.'

I've been in bed with lovers and have apologised for my belly and my scars. The thing is, I know they don't care because orgasms are more powerful than any mark on my body. My scars are a testament to my survival. I started calling them 'beauty marks' in my teens. Men are told 'Chicks dig scars', but I've never heard anyone say, 'Men dig scars.' Over time, I have come to feel a profound affection for my scars and how they are worn into my skin like an old lightning strike on a tree. These indentations on my body symbolise my survivorship and they tell me – and others – that I just might skate on the surface of being a warrior.

Ever since I can remember, the only person I've been able to trust and grab on to has been myself. When I feel too heavy for others to carry, I wrap one hand around my wrist like a tourniquet until I feel my pulse thrumming and whisper, 'You're okay, you're okay' like an invocation; as mantra, as prayer. I tell myself I'll be okay as long as I survive the next disaster, and this becomes something of a bargaining tool for when I can't get through on silent will alone. I want to ask how other people deal with this type of trauma but then I remember that everyone I want to ask is dead.

Traumatic experiences linked to the body often can't be talked through. These deeply somatic experiences can't be articulated because they simply transcend language. During my book research I learn how childhood trauma is intrinsically linked to addiction in later life, and while I had always known that my childhood was an anomaly, things begin to make sense when I receive an official diagnosis of complex post-traumatic stress disorder (C-PTSD). I don't feel anything like validation, possibly because it's always been in plain sight.

An endless cycle of trauma ruptures a person's spirit and while I try to understand *what* has happened to me, I have always wanted to know *why*. But it's hard to ascertain when I'm dealing with elements outside my control like genetics and the unwieldy trajectory of a terminal illness. You can't outrun genetics, you can't outrun a lifetime of trauma, and there is no coming back from C-PTSD when it's punched into every cell of your being. Some days I'm completely unaware it even exists. But then I hear a song, or think of a word, and it doesn't so much bubble to the surface but lurches through my body and I am back in that moment, or at least, the memory of that moment.

All my senses – sight, taste, touch, sound, smell – get stuck in the time and place of a particular memory. The smell of an alcohol wipe rips me back to being held down and repeatedly cannulated as a child. The smell of Milton disinfectant brings to mind nasal gastric tubes being forced up my nose until I bled. Remembrances can be an everyday occurrence, so I've always wanted to know, why, then, do I remember as much as I do? Unlike some trauma survivors, I don't have gaps in my memory – only the very detailed minutiae of what has been left behind.

I'm not anti-therapy, but after having a forced relationship with it in early childhood it compounds every awful feeling, which is why talk therapy has been the most harmful and reckless 'healing modality' I've ever used. When I told a psychiatrist I had been seeing for about three years that I didn't want to live, she said, 'I think you're doing really well' and sent me home. I immediately terminated the relationship.

It's now widely accepted that talk therapy is contraindicated for people with acute and chronic PTSD. In its place is trauma-informed care – a framework based on acknowledging the impact of trauma and creating personalised pathways for recovery by actively avoiding re-traumatisation.

One psychologist I saw was an Eye Movement Desensitisation Reprocessing (EMDR) specialist, and although I only had one session, it did more for me than any therapist had ever done when I was able to process one of my most traumatic memories of an incident in ICU after my transplant. No-one tells you how crucial a role the adrenal gland plays.

I'm astounded I still have a pulse, with the stress hormones that have flooded my body and brain over the course of my life. I've come to realise that what I experienced when I was wheeled, howling, into theatre – that clarion call for my dying (or was it for my life?) – was collapse. My body sensed that death was imminent and so it went numb and limp. It felt like someone had pulled my heart through my stomach with a hook, and all I could hear was a loud buzzing sound, like that moment of ultimate surrender and peace before you yield to general anaesthesia. The brain is the ultimate emergency system – kind of like an internal smoke alarm – but instead of fighting or trying to scramble off the gurney, I completely shut down.

I read years later that once a person experiences the fight, flight or freeze response in a life-threatening situation, it never leaves the body. Instead, it lives on and repeatedly resurfaces in your day-to-day life. Called false-positive bias, it's when every unfamiliar moment is braided with terror.

⚘

After breaking off several teeth in my sleep, in 2020 I acquiesce to wearing a mouthguard. I have bruxism, which is the involuntary grinding and clenching of teeth. If you clench or grind your teeth during the day, it's at least six times worse when you're asleep. I tell my dentist that it feels like my teeth are far shorter than they were two years ago.

'The enamel on your teeth isn't great, and you've got four wisdom teeth that need to come out.'

I nearly throw up. I have an irrational fear of dental work, and my mind harks back to when my friends were all having their wisdom teeth removed and I felt smug for having got away without having to have surgery. I remember ice packs strapped to their swollen faces as they spat blood into kidney dishes, looking entirely miserable.

But my dentist is lovely and gentle as he tells me I'll probably need a maxillofacial surgeon to remove the wayward teeth. For the second time that day, I nearly vomit all over his shoes. He shows me the X-ray, and I see where my teeth are trying to push through my gums, as well as the area of decay in my back molar. More telling are the criss-cross patterns I see up close on my teeth from the litany of grinding.

'I don't know what else to do,' I say.

He knows I'm talking about my PTSD.

'There are people who specialise in this kind of thing – trauma and how it relates to your teeth.'

'Like a therapist for my teeth?'

'Kind of,' he says, and we both laugh. 'I'm so sorry this is happening to you. You've already been through way too much.'

I make another appointment, walk back to my car, and cry. I haven't had private health insurance since I was twenty-one, and the cost of the kind of mouthguard I need is twelve hundred dollars. Then there's the surgery. I opt to go on a public waiting list and hope for the best. If my parents couldn't pay for my medical bills, I don't know where I'd be. I feel like a piece of shit for being so upset about something so trivial when one of my CF transplant friends is dying of liver cancer. Mum and Nikki tell me that I should perhaps take my own advice of 'it's all relative' and to stop comparing my molehills to other people's mountains. But it's easier said than done when you've gone through your entire life as the queen of invalidating your own suffering. If I were a Mr Men book, I'd be *Little Miss It Can Always Be Worse.*

Three weeks later, my beloved friend Peebo dies. I keep repeating as mantra, as prayer, 'It can always be worse.'

It is said that everyone has a superpower. Mine is listening, and I come to see this as something I can use in service to others. In the late 2000s, I become a self-appointed 'death midwife'. I'm a lifelong practitioner of grief and see it as a life-affirming event. I think about death a lot, which is to say, I think a lot about life. My training has been a lifetime of experience looking after and seeing out the dying. I had long wanted to work in palliative care because I wanted to help people. Perhaps a small part of me thought I could befriend death. And if I could befriend death, I could beat it at its own game.

In 2014 I start a death midwifery course with renowned palliative care physician Doctor Michael Barbato, and Deathwalker training with Natural Death Care Centre founder Zenith Virago. The world of hospital chaplaincy opens up for me after I attend a Spiritual Care Australia conference in Adelaide, and I apply to do a three-month clinical pastoral-care intensive at Brisbane's biggest trauma hospital. I cry with relief when I'm accepted into the program, and on a feverishly hot February day in 2015, with a group of people from differing faith backgrounds, I descend into the hospital basement.

There's a Presbyterian, an Anglican, a French Buddhist, a Seventh Day Adventist and a Uniting Church deacon. Then there's me, the agnostic. The group is curious and confounded as to why I want to be a hospital chaplain. After we meet each other, our supervisor takes us to the wards and leaves us to fend for ourselves. Meeting people – patients – on our first day is immersive and oddly terrifying, but I manage to emerge feeling not so much victorious as useful. Over the course of my training, I realise that it's not my role to help, even though that's what I want to do. Instead, I hold space for people. I hold their hand and listen. And while it might not sound like much, I am told it is everything.

When I need to debrief after my second shift in emergency, I'm grateful that our supervisor is one of the best mentors I've ever had. I need to debrief not because of what I see but what I hear.

Each student in emergency has a supervising chaplain. Over the course of the night, my chaplain repeatedly questions why I am here.

'Who do you belong to?' she asks, scoffing her first cheese toastie of the night.

'I'm sorry?'

She lets out a breath of exasperation, a vanishing point to happiness. 'What faith group do you belong to?'

'I belong to myself.'

'So, you're not part of a church?'

She's slow. 'I'm not, no.'

'And you're doing pastoral care?'

'I am.'

Her body jounces wildly as she huffs and rolls her eyes, as though she is hearing about some war atrocity. Anne makes more cheese toasties during our shift and doesn't do any pastoral care. We walk around the emergency department once, even after there has been an influx of patients who could use a chat. Later in the night, a social worker barrels into the room where we're sitting. A call has come through that a young girl has been in a car crash.

Her mother and grandfather have been killed on impact, and first responders can't ascertain how old she is. It turns out she's fourteen, and she's being flown by helicopter to the nearest adult hospital, which just happens to be ours.

'Oh, terrible,' says my supervisor between bites of her toastie.

I know stress can make people hungry but fuck me, this is something else.

'Well, there's nothing we can do,' says Anne.

Throughout the night, my supervising chaplain softens a little. She shows me photos of her grandchildren, and I show her pictures of my nephews in exchange for a basic modicum of respect. We make small talk while folding a pile of donated clothes so people have something to wear when they go home, should theirs be cut off when they come into emergency.

Despite this rapprochement, I'm still shocked by her behaviour. The job requires a level of tact that Anne didn't have. You have to remember that hospitals are places of worry and angst. People are in surgery, people are having potentially life-altering tests and are waiting for results that may shorten or end their lives or shorten or end the life of their loved one. Compassion is key.

⸸

During my first week of training, I'm visiting the head and neck ward when I'm asked to see an elderly gentleman by the name of Ivan.

'Just watch yourself. He's been pretty aggro with some of the nurses.'

'Pissed off is my specialty,' I say, with a wink.

I make no judgement and walk to where he is at the end of the ward – as though he's been secreted away. I find him alone in a four-bed room, propped up on uncomfortable plastic pillows in the dark, his hospital gown askew, and half of his head missing. I later learn that plastic surgeons are in the process of reconstructing his head after invasive skin cancer. His nose and one of his eyes are covered by thick pieces of flesh from the back of his head, and there are chunks of skin missing from his face. He's groggy from a morphine infusion, and the eye he can see out of is so swollen it looks like a bloodied laceration. He later tells me that I looked delightfully fuzzy, like an angel.

I introduce myself, and he invites me to sit beside him. The man speaks to me in a gentle, lilting voice, falling asleep every few minutes. I observe the cadence of his breath, watching over him until he wakes up and begins to speak again. It's clear from our conversation that no-one has been listening to him and that he is in both physical and existential agony. I'd be fucking cranky, too.

'You're good to go and see him,' says a nurse on my way out. 'He's actually really lovely.'

'Oh.'

I can't fault the care of the nurses. In an understaffed ward where care at the bedside is in short supply, I know they are doing their best.

Over several visits, Ivan and I have unexpectedly philosophical conversations. One day he tells me about his brother who had been killed in a motorcycle accident at the age of nineteen – a loss his father never got over. As proud men who worked the land, they would rather cut off their hands than talk about their emotions.

'I've never told anyone this. I hope it's okay if I tell you?'

'Of course, it is. You can tell me whatever you want to, okay?'

Over the next five weeks we get to know each other, and with each visit, Ivan is less drowsy and shares more about his life. Finally, on our last encounter, he is sitting up in bed in his pyjamas, his face back in one piece.

'I'm going home,' he says, jumping out of bed with a little jig.

He takes my hand in his and thanks me.

'It's been an honour, kind sir,' I say.

When I get home that afternoon, I unlock my front door and burst into tears.

⚘

When people ask me how I find meaning, I tell them that I find meaning in purpose. When I leave for the day after a shift, I don't take my pastoral care hat off until I walk through my front door. I lose count of the times people tell me their life story in the hospital car park when I'm helping them with their parking ticket.

One morning, as I'm rushing out of the spinal injuries unit, there's a man in a wheelchair sobbing. He's a big guy – tall and weighty – and his arms are festooned in tattoos. One is a swastika. He is a sticky mess of spittle and tears, and I can't leave him on his own.

'Hey, I'm CJ.'

'Hi. I'm … I'm Daniel.' He sniffs.

'What's going on, mate?'

I sit level with him because I've never been comfortable with the power imbalance between patient and carer. He tells me he's not adjusting to being a paraplegic and he feels like he's let his kids down. He's also in the full throes of morphine withdrawal.

'You know,' he says, between wiping strings of snot from his nose, 'if you hadn't've come and talked to me, I was going to fuckin' throw myself down those stairs. You saved my life.'

'I'm really glad you didn't do that.'

'Yeah, me too. Me wife would've fuckin' killed me.'

It's only as I'm leaving that I notice that the stairs he was just talking about are edged with stainless steel. I suggest to the nursing unit manager that they might want to get the staircase blocked off with a locked gate.

Later that week, I share this with the class as a critical incident, and when I go to see Daniel again, he and his family are sitting in the sunshine talking and laughing over an impromptu picnic.

'Daniel, my man!'

'CJ! Look – it's my guardian angel,' he says to his wife and kids.

I sit down and listen as his kids tell me about school and show me photos of their friends.

Life is a never-ending cycle of grief and learning. Some encounters begin with people yelling at me to get out of their room just because I say I'm from pastoral care.

'I don't want to talk about fucking religion!'

'Neither do I,' I say, which always piques their curiosity.

'But you're a chaplain.'

'I'm not religious.'

'How does that work? Won't you try and convert me?'

'The only conversion I'm interested in is the one we lost last night in the second half of the State of Origin.' For some reason, a lot of people want to talk about football.

After the initial scepticism, I find that everyone is spiritual about something. For men, it's often their dog (I get that), their farm, truck or shed. For women, it's their pet, craft, cooking or garden. Everyone is spiritual about music. When they tell me about what means the most to them, I tell them that just because they're not religious, it doesn't mean they're spiritually stymied. It cracks open some profound conversations I can never predict. It's a privilege being in service to others when I've always been the one being looked after, and I relish this strange duality.

Towards the end of my tenure as a student chaplain, I meet a man in his thirties on the orthopaedic ward who is spiritual about his truck. Or at least, he was spiritual about his truck until another driver deliberately drove into it as an act of suicide. He tells me about the crash and how it left him in a coma for three weeks. Both of his legs are in pieces, and he has severe internal injuries for which he was on life support in ICU.

In pastoral care, we're taught to ask open-ended questions, but I can feel this man's anguish, and so I ask what happened to the other driver.

'He's dead.'

'Oh.'

'I'm glad the cunt's dead. He got what he wanted and left me to die on the side of the road like a dog.'

He's angry, but it's not anger stained with bitterness. It's a sense of confusion and sadness I can see imbuing his every thought. We talk about his life before the crash, and he hands me his phone to show me photos of his wrecked prime mover.

'Holy shit,' I say. 'So, do people say that you're lucky?' I ask him, handing him back his phone.

'Yeah. And I should be grateful.'

'Why should you?'

'Because I'm alive.'

'You have every right to be pissed off and to not feel lucky, you know,' I say.

'I dunno how I feel yet. It depends on how well I can function after rehab, which is gonna take months.'

'You deserve to feel angry, but you deserve to heal and have a future, too. Do you think maybe you're being a bit hard on yourself?'

At this, his bottom lip quivers and he begins to cry. I hold his hand, and we shoulder the silence together. The world stops for a moment, and I feel a shift in this parallel to my own life.

⚘

At the beginning of my training, I question whether it's my job to help patients realise and acknowledge their spirituality. The answer to that question is no. It's my role to listen and support my patients, and should they want to explore their spirituality, I'm able to create a space and hold open the door for these conversations. My role is not to convert people.

Whenever I meet a new patient, I always joke that I've been tasked with looking after the heathens, and this never fails to raise a smile or a, 'Hey, that's me!' It's an ever-evolving body of care, and there's not a single shift where I don't learn something – about myself or others, or both. When I arrive at the hospital each morning I head up to the pastoral care department with a heaving sense of purpose. I feel part of something greater than myself. I'm welcomed into the department by whoever is there, and before I do my rounds I chat to the other chaplains. It's a place that has a rich diversity of faiths – Anglican, Baha'i, Baptist, Buddhist, Catholic, Muslim, Seventh Day Adventist, Sikh – and I always feel heartened that should there be a problem to solve or if the chaplains need to be listened to, I am included.

Towards the end of our training, our little cohort is invited to share something 'big' that has happened in our lives. There are stories of sexual abuse, familial alienation for pursuing a passion, the feeling of never being good enough, and secret abortions. I tussle with sharing my history of addiction, and for my trouble, I feel ill all day. I end up sharing it with the group, and some of them are in tears as I speak.

The following week, I'm having breakfast with my closest childhood friend. Bec knows about the survivor's guilt I've grappled with.

'What's it like being on the other side of the bed?' she asks.

'It kind of feels like I've come home.'

She nods, full of knowing.

'I feel like I'm actively atoning to my donor and her family. Sounds ridiculous, but that's how it feels,' I say, with a sense of perverse pride, knowing full well that nothing will ever assuage my guilt.

⸸

A couple of months after I start my pastoral care training, I get a phone call from Dad about his mother. Again, we find ourselves in the gentle footfalls of death.

'It's Nana. She hasn't got long.'

I drive to the nursing home where my grandfather Arthur died, and walk in to see Nana – Gladdy – on her bed. She's in the foetal position, just like how a baby lays within its mother's womb. Dad is all red-faced and wet-cheeked. I hug him, then go over to hold Nana's hand. I eventually hop into the bed with her, nursing her body as she takes her final, peaceful breaths.

'Last of the Mohicans,' says Dad, trying to be stoic.

I think of all the times she held me – as a baby, giving me physio on her ironing board, making me cups of tea, and holding me in her love – and I feel humbled that I can be here to give this last act of love and devotion to her.

Uncle David arrives not long after Nana dies, and he tells us that a photograph of her that's been in the back of his truck for years blew across his windscreen at the time she left this world. For the next year, I smell the familiar scent of cigarette smoke and lavender in my apartment, even with the doors closed. There are no known smokers in the building. I see the spectre of my grandmother chain-smoking in the corner of my living room and remember all the times she threw back her head in peals of laughter as she told me to never get married.

⸸

My dad was a big believer in natural therapies and took me to naturopaths over the years. The treatment would work for a while, and then I'd plateau. I'd feel better for a few months, and then my protocol would be changed again. As well as natural therapies, I always seemed to be on the cusp of breakthrough treatments like Pulmozyme – a nebulised drug that helps cut through long strands of CF mucus, so it makes the mucus thinner and easier to cough up. It essentially cleaves our sticky DNA into pieces. This drug wasn't immediately subsidised by the pharmaceutical benefits scheme, so I was fortunate enough that my parents could afford to buy it at around the cost of $1000 a month. It had to be stored in an esky, so when we went to the USA in 1996 my mum somehow managed to keep it cool and my dad wrangled me into nebulising the stuff twice a day. I think this speaks of my parents' dedication to keeping me alive.

In 2022, my transplant team tell me I'm a perfect candidate for CF miracle drug Trikafta – a medication primarily used in pre-transplant CFs. At a cost of $300,000 a year, it is now subsidised, so all CFs can access it. My quality of life had been poor due to constant infection in my sinuses. Every year, I would have major sinus surgery where surgeons would drill into my nasal passages to create more drainage and remove the bunches of polyps that are a trait of CF. Despite the surgery, I was debilitated by headaches and migraines nearly every day. I go into my Trikafta experience with no expectations, and it cures my sinus issues. My ENT surgeons are amazed.

'Where is all the snot?' they ask at my first post-surgery appointment after starting the drug.

Trikafta has given me my life back. I always said that I was born at the right time with having benefitted (fleetingly) from Pulmozyme, then lung transplantation, and advances in immunosuppression drugs, and now Trikafta. Now people born with CF are going to live into their eighties without the need for a lung transplant. I never thought I would see this happen in my lifetime.

And yet, life after transplant isn't happily ever after. It's not a cure – it's more of a stop gap. My stop gap has somehow turned into twenty-five years of life. I can't pinpoint an exact time where I felt healed. I always felt that there was a wound. I felt fallow, never complete, and I still do. With morbidity rates being so high when I had my transplant, my family and I hoped I would have maybe five years. Anything after that was a bonus. Then I made it to a decade, and that was after cancer nearly took me out. Soon, it was fifteen, twenty – every day feels like a permutation of a gift and something of a fever dream. In the end, I've come away with far more than I have given, and far more than I've lost. I have come away with my life. Over the years, there are scares of rejection and mycobacterium and with this, there is a panic that glides into my body seamlessly, like a ribbon being pulled through a loop.

I WAS BORN TO LIVE, and I was born to die.

Say that to yourself right now.

Now, say it again.

I was born to live, and I was born to die.

It's one thing to say it, but another to believe or accept it. The only thing promised to us in life, is death, and it's no secret that our culture – in the West, at least – has a deep-seated phobia of dying and death. For many people, it comes as a complete surprise that they will die. We live in a death-denying and deeply death phobic culture, and it's only recently that death literacy has become framed in a public health context.

Life is about continual regeneration and destruction. The human body turns over roughly 330 billion cells every day, which is a colossal feat of nature. Life is also about choice, and this is one of the reasons I went into pastoral care – because patients who don't subscribe to religion or any 'officially' recognised belief system don't have a choice who they get to see should they need spiritual counsel. When I turned eighteen, the hospital I transitioned to was Catholic, so my choice was limited to Catholic priests, nuns and volunteers. The last person I wanted to speak to when I was either sick, dying or recovering was a person affiliated with a church. I had heard horror stories of deathbed conversions, and while I wasn't concerned about that, it would have been helpful to speak to someone about the pressing matter of dying. After all, it's not death that's hard – it's the dying. Death was never scary for me, but the dying always has been. It's well documented that once a person's existential or spiritual angst has been alleviated, there is less need for pain medication. Again, it's the terror: the terror of not knowing, the terror of having no choice, the terror of it hurting, the terror of being forgotten.

The thing about choice, though, is that it's often a privilege. As an adolescent, my CF friends and I had conversations about euthanasia, and we were all in favour of it long before I became aware of one of my heroes, Doctor Philip Nitschke. I've always been passionate about having the right to die because it *is* a right, although it's treated as something of a luxury that can only happen in some sort of death utopia. Hospital was, and still is, one of the last places I want to die. The terror I felt upon nearly dying in 2007 is something that took me years to shake loose. I've spoken to my mate David 'Dagwood' Bissell about what our dream death would look like, and it looks a lot like this: we're sitting on a beach at sunset surrounded by our friends and family under fairy lights as we sip cocktails that have been prepped with a fatal dose of pentobarbital. Wild fantasies aside, I want the choice about when to end my life, as well as how and by what means.

Why should my death – or anyone else's – be mandated by church or state? If I didn't have long to live, my hope would be to die at home, surrounded by my loved ones and my dog. I want wine and music and people to hyper-salivate over food (grief makes you hungry) and all of the beauty that comes with that.

The myth that palliative care is a panacea for suffering is a mistruth. The medical fraternity want us to believe that every illness can be palliated effectively, and this feels like a profound betrayal to me. It's also a systemic betrayal. There is an endless list of things that can happen to a human body when we're dying, and most of them aren't pretty: terminal restlessness, pain that can't be controlled with the standard pharmaceutical pain medications, chronic constipation that leads to agonising bowel obstructions, and delirium.

When my aunt is dying of cancer in 2019, she has uncontrollable pain and terminal restlessness. Because of the pandemic, I can't visit her in hospital, so through my mum I suggest that the doctors give her midazolam – a powerful benzodiazepine that is often used before you're given general anaesthetic for surgery. No-one on the palliative care team had brought up any such option. Thankfully, it worked for my aunt and while she may not have wanted to die via voluntary assisted dying, she should have had the choice.

If there is a victor, surely it is death that triumphs over medicine. Sometimes, illness is not a great riddle to be solved. Sometimes it just is. Death isn't always profound or beautiful, or peaceful. Sometimes it's dying in agony as you shit the bed while your kids look on in horror.

I'm no expert, but I can guarantee most people will die one of two ways. They're either going to die well or very, very badly. We all know the power of being the steward of our own lives, so why don't we do this in death? We have birth plans, but never a death plan. The death phobia that pervades our culture has been responsible for so much suffering, much of it avoidable. Having a death plan isn't being histrionic or morbid. It's practical and a good lesson in being kind to yourself and your loved ones.

Thankfully in 2023, voluntary assisted dying (VAD) became legal in the state of Queensland, but it's a flimsy platform to pin your hopes on. You need to be of sound mind to go through the assessment to be approved for VAD, and I find myself catastrophising about a situation where I am left in a severely disabled state with no hope of an exit plan where I can die by my own hand.

⚘

As a patient, a human and a spiritual carer, the over-treatment of illness concerns me. To my horror, after my best friend's father dies, I find out he was still being given trial immunotherapy the week before his death at five thousand dollars a pop. The word 'dying' was not once mentioned by his oncologist, and it was only because of a passing remark by a nurse that my friend and her sisters realised he was at the end of his life. It was not so much a miscommunication as an absolute non-conversation. I find myself feeling furious on behalf of my friend and her family, overshadowed by a profound sense of sadness that they thought they had more time, or worse – that there was hope. In the end, it was up to me to tell her that her dad didn't have weeks – he had days.

Just like death, the idea of 'conquering illness' is profoundly embedded in our culture. And if we can't beat it, let's hide it. Palliative care takes its name from 'pall', which means to shroud, to hide. We hide from death as though it's something to be ashamed of. We hide from death because we think we can outwit it.

It's clear, yet disappointing, that little has changed in the twenty-five years since my own doctors failed to mention dying – a fact that still astounds me. But then I ask myself, is it really that surprising, given our rampant death phobia? Sadly, it is not. Our refusal to die is not life affirming. This grudge we have against endings is a betrayal. For me, death is the unavoidable truth of our lives. Stephen Jenkinson, who runs the Orphan Wisdom school from his farm in rural Ontario, thinks the problem lies on a deeper level. Jenkinson holds Master's degrees in theology and social work from Harvard and the University of Toronto. In his 2015 book *Die Wise*, he writes that what Western people suffer from most is 'culture failure, amnesia of ancestry and deep family story, phantom or sham rites of passage, no instruction on how to live with each other or with the world around us or with our dead or with our history'.

After working in what he calls 'the death trade' for nearly three decades, he created the Orphan Wisdom school, where people from all around the world come together to learn about life, dying, death, community and elderhood. In the 2008 documentary *Griefwalker*, Jenkinson says, 'The crucible of making human beings is death. Every culture worth a damn knows that. It's not success, it's not growth, it's not happiness – it's death. That's the cradle of your love of life – the fact that it ends.'

Every time I hear these words, a jolt of warmth unfurls down my spine. They bring me such comfort. It ends. This all ends. Jenkinson summarises what I've seen time and time again. While our physical pain can mostly be managed, he sees the terror, or what he calls the 'wretched anxiety', in the dying. Where physical symptoms are mostly alleviated by psychotropic pain drugs, spiritual and existential pain and suffering isn't something that can be vanquished with pharmaceuticals, and I've seen treatment become trauma so often. With the overtreatment of illness, we're both prolonging life and prolonging death, which only prolongs suffering, and I cannot think of a worse place to be.

⚘

Funerals are often big, redemptive affairs that are all about cost. All cost, no meaning. We have handed over the most sacred experiences of our lives to people we do not know and companies we do not trust. What I want to know is this: How do we honour

our dead when we live in a culture that wants quick, clean cuts from anything to do with death? How do I honour my dead when I've grown up in a culture that distils the life of a person – be they child or adult – into a one-hour service while the next family waits to farewell their loved one in another cookie-cutter sixty-minute service? Why aren't we doing more for our dead? Why do we not honour the grief that we feel and bear witness to? How do you distil the life of a human child into a one-hour service with a eulogy and a slideshow of photos that's bookended by two songs? How can we do this better and why aren't we doing it better?

As it turns out, some people are doing it better.

Some people have left big funeral homes to create their own bespoke farewell experiences, like the not-for-profit Tender Funerals that started in Port Kembla. Tender Funerals is a community-led funeral service model. They have learnt how to stay present with death and are reclaiming the rituals surrounding the end of life, and this has fostered conversations around dying and death. They can arrange to care for your dying loved one at home and have resources like cooling plates so if a person does die at home, family and friends have the time and space to spend with their loved one, which is what our ancestors used to do in the family parlour. They would lay out their dead, take photographs and spend time with their loved one. Tender Funerals do funeral planning, arrange wills, and have funeral services that are affordable and unique. They have created an alternative to the funeral homes that are owned by the one multinational based in America. It's a funeral service model with none of the bullshit or hard sell.

It's as though the death industry likes to have us existing in this fugue-like state where we're barely cognisant of the decisions we're making because we're so rooted in the depths of despair at the most impossible time of our lives. I lament our loss of ritual and ceremony because it is sacred. I lament our loss of ritual and ceremony because it is ours. Collective grief isn't something we do well, and we could learn from our First Nations people who grieve as a community and let the emotions move through them. Everyone has a role in sorry business – there's ritual, ceremony, reverence, and mourners are truly present in their grief. I hope that one day we can reclaim our grief. People talk about it, yet most people don't actually do it, because they've never looked at grief beyond the prism that has been prescribed to us. Colonisation and the resultant stiff upper lip have not served us well. I find it shocking that 'excessive' mourning was seen as indulgent and even as mental illness in Victorian England.

It doesn't matter what we die from, but *how* we die. Death became a medicalised event in the early twentieth century, but death is anything but medical. It's cultural, psychosocial, spiritual and human and as such should be anchored in humanity. Spiritual events are often not spectacular, but they exist. The supernatural exists – and by supernatural, I mean the event is natural but it's on steroids, so to speak.

Ironically, it's dying children who think they've led a full life, whereas adults rail against their end – usually of the things undone and unsaid. Kids are a bullshit-free zone. They accept because they haven't learnt the strangling behaviours, and one of those things is that to have a meaningful life it must be a long one. I look at my friend Ineka and her impact on people. She might have only been fifteen when she died, yet she planned her own funeral and what she wanted written on her epitaph. Most adults can't even go there in their minds.

We are drunk on youth. We have an addiction to staying young and looking young, but more than this, we are obsessed with staying alive at any cost. Progress is often seen as moving forward. But for me, progress is about looking backwards, and by that, I mean deeply examining experience and the old ways. By the old ways, I am talking about respecting nature and our elders where death was once a part of everyday life. I'm talking about harvest and the cycle of the moon, taking notice of the seasons and how growing old was once revered and is now seen as an embarrassment. Sometimes it's not in the picking up – it's in the putting down and in the leaving behind.

We are deluded from an early age into believing we're in control. If there is one thing life is devoid of, it's control. Wisdom and experience are two different things. Not everything needs to be a lesson or a teachable moment, and suffering is not necessarily a conduit to wisdom. You don't find meaning out of everything. What if we were okay with that?

Contemporary Western culture is nowhere near where it needs to be when it comes to death literacy. We need to learn how to be fluent in death. It is a language we need to learn, and there is grace in this. We ignore it when we should be sitting beside it. Instead, fantastical euphemisms give us room to move further away from the truth.

I will not *pass away*. I will die. I will not *lose the fight*. I will die. I will not *slip away*. I will die. I will not *succumb*. I will die. I will not *reach the end*. I will die. We are addicted to little hits of dopamine, and we've overinvested in a culture that doesn't believe in dying and where death is seen as a failure. But it's not. Dying is the most natural thing in the world, bookended only by birth. We like to think it doesn't happen to everyone, especially to the people we love, but it always has and always will and I think there's beauty in that tiny kernel of certainty. Dying is something that happens *to* you.

The miracle isn't treatment at the eleventh hour. The miracle is the natural order of things, when we can die without our loved ones telling us to 'fight' or hold on. I am only here because of medical intervention – surgery, medication, life-preserving procedures – but I like to think I would know when to go gently into that good night. My interest lies in how we can shift what's currently seen as a medical event into one that is more connected to humanity.

In the age of medical miracles, opinion is divided on when to stop treatment. Are they life-preserving, or just extra time for suffering? We don't 'do' death – we're hopeless at it – and historically, doctors do not like to lose. Death is a failure. In 2017, I'm on a panel at the Spiritual Care Australia conference when a Catholic chaplain (also a retired doctor) disagrees with me about doctors feeling like failures when patients don't survive.

'Oh nonsense!' he says. 'We never felt like we failed.'

This doctor would have been practising in the 1960s when medicine was cold and impersonal. I speak about the discussions I've had with my own doctors and with friends who are doctors who have divulged that they *did* feel as though they'd failed their patients who had died. Conference delegates approach me for the rest of the day, sharing that they, too, had had similar conversations and experiences.

Doctors were experts at dehumanising patients when I was growing up in the 1980s, to the point where I thought they were taught a special course in it at medical school. All they saw were the symptoms and the next course of treatment. Never the person. All they saw was a body in a bed, and they were more focused on outcomes, even if those outcomes were terrible. Because there are fates worse than death.

They were so hyper-focused on trying to fix us that we were distilled into one generic person in our identical steel beds. But I also feel that my doctors saw so much suffering and death on such an immense scale that they had no other choice but to compartmentalise. It was easier to see us as a patient and not a person; as a human Petri dish or collection of symptoms to control and conquer. We were the by-products of our disease and the system. Healing never came into the equation because medicine was about fixing and curing. Not once did I ever hear the word 'heal' when I was growing up.

Dehumanisation is now mercifully rare because doctors are more adept at dealing with the nuance of what is it to be human. Their communication skills have risen above the culture of stoicism and silence where they're able to connect with their patients. A great example is a question now often asked in palliative care: 'What are your goals?' I believe this question to be prudent in every other medical situation.

Growing up, the medical dynamic could feel disempowering – especially with doctors who weren't permanent fixtures on the CF team. I would find my sense of self diminished because I felt like a medical specimen – a pin cushion, a body to observe and inflict pain on. I rarely felt this way with my CF consultants. It was the residents and registrars that ebbed and flowed between rotations who inflicted the most damage.

It's little wonder patients lose their identity as human beings because people are hyper-focused on fixing what is 'wrong'. It was always up to me to hold on to and even claw at who I was so I could stay tethered to myself. I'll say it again: 'healing' was never mentioned. It was a word I never heard. 'Cure', on the other hand, was often the subject of conversation.

As a patient, you're on a constant learning curve with your interpersonal skills to bridge the cleft between you, your disease and your treating doctors, and I understand the benefits to dehumanising or dissociating from patients. I know some doctors didn't see 'me' – just my lungs because that's the organ that needed care and attention. They saw an X-ray or what was colonising in my sputum. And while we want our doctors to know we're more than our organs and body parts, it's easy to forget they are also human. Sometimes, doctors need to be healed, too.

The most important thing – for them and us – is that we actually do need them to be clinical and unfeeling when it comes to preserving our lives. It is their lightning-fast problem-solving skills that saves lives, so for me at least, I no longer care whether I'm being treated like a specimen. In the midst of a medical emergency, just save my fucking life – please.

JUST LIKE THE WORD 'HEALING', the word 'trauma' was never used in the same lexicon as CF when I was growing up. In fact, it wasn't a term I heard until many years after my transplant. As I got older, I accepted that I was so traumatised and psychologically brittle that I could split apart at any time. And I did – often. It's just that very few people knew. Having been anchored in survival mode for most of my life, I've come to understand that chronic trauma experienced over a lifetime is a different beast from being exposed to a single or even multiple traumatic events. No-one ever spoke to me about post-traumatic stress. It just didn't exist or wasn't extant within the context of illness. My friends and I were never offered counselling despite being at the epicentre of extreme suffering, dying and death as children. We were just expected to get on with it without a backwards glance. With a childhood steeped in grief, I'd been insulated by suffering; tragedy pummelled me into compliance. I always felt I was being punished, though I was never sure of the crime. For anyone without the full picture it must seem utterly Kafkaesque. Robert Frost wrote in his poem 'A Servant to Servants': *the best way out is always through.* For me, the only way out is *in.* While I've been able to apply a kind of radical acceptance to some parts of my life, I've found death and acceptance make odd bedfellows.

For me, love, hope and faith have been the triumvirate that have liberated me from despair. Grief is a song on my skin and a fire in my heart. It is everything, yet it is nothing. I have experienced relationships forged in grief, and they have been some of my most life-affirming, for loss binds us to the human condition. Grief is also an oddly ubiquitous beast that likes to take up residence in every corner of our lives. I have lived with it my whole life, and we are old foes; but I am still at sea struggling to navigate it after nearly half a century.

I've questioned whether this book is wanted or needed in the canon of memoir. But then I consider that there is a slew of grief memoirs out in the world for good reason. They not only speak to people grieving death, but they also speak to those of us who are constantly grappling with loss – the loss of loved ones, relationships, outcomes we'd been expecting, identities, and even our bodily functions. And while this may be a never-ending cycle, there is a staid passion in it. There is passion in remembering, and there is passion in having lost something or someone we love. For better or worse, age deepens grief. Time does nothing to dilute it.

In 2018, when I'm researching complex trauma, what I want to know is this – is it possible to structurally repair memory?

Growing up, I was protected in the arms of strangers who became friends – my nurses. But with that came a strange dichotomy of being helped and being hurt. I automatically assume my beloved nurses have PTSD, and although my CF friends gave me solace, our friendships were routinely truncated, becoming another source of grief.

Living with CF was akin to being a spy and leading a double life. I would turn it on and off when I was with my friends, in social situations, and especially in 'normal' school. Learning was my escape. Throughout primary and secondary school, I basically had to keep my shit together – more for other people than myself. And so, there was home, and there was hospital. But like any good spy, I could move seamlessly from hospital to 'normal' without giving it a second thought. It helped that my disease was essentially invisible. I never *looked* sick: my weight was uncharacteristically stable for someone with CF, and my skin glowed with a summer tan.

I don't know why I survived. It certainly doesn't come down to a certain level of strength or the will to live. I've known so many other kids with a stronger constitution than me who were more determined to live but did not. In the unfairness of life, it all comes down to luck, compliance, knowing your limits. Of all the things that have nearly killed me, the existential suffering caused by a tsunami of grief was perhaps the most perilous. I had to relearn how to live after I nearly died. It felt like a rite of passage no-one else had ever experienced, or a journey there was no map for, and for so long afterwards, I became waylaid.

I have learnt that grief does not end – it is fluid. It is not something you get over – it is something you learn to live around. Grief is the kind of beast that's never heard of a sabbatical. There is no such thing as 'closure' or 'moving on'. At its most basic, closure is a fallacy and, at its most intricate, a fantasy. I haven't moved on. I don't want to move on. There is no heart-warming or neat ending. It's full of loose and messy threads, yet we *do* go on. We press on, we persist. And we often do this to our detriment, as we try to convince ourselves and everyone else that we are okay.

The truth is, we are born grieving. We arrive in a wet, bloody, screaming mess as we're cast from our mother's body. This is our first loss – that of the dark and still amniotic sac that has been our home for nine months. Where has that soft, silent place gone?

Humans are in a constant state of grief. Every loss we endure is a form of death, and we grieve that loss. But grief is not being without joy; they can co-exist. They *do* co-exist. I am living proof of this.

⚘

In *Illness as Metaphor*, Susan Sontag wrote that for people living with illness, there is a 'before' and 'after'. You're either in the kingdom of the well or the sick. Being born with an incurable illness meant I was quite literally delivered into the kingdom of the sick when my mother birthed me. Where so many memoirs about illness begin with, 'My life was wonderful UNTIL . . .', my story begins in the womb. While I've had moments of clarity and joy, I've never had long periods of time where life has been unhindered by my disease. I find it difficult to imagine what it would feel like to be well for months or years at a time and not having regular doctors' appointments or having to go to the chemist every week.

I never had an 'old' life to reclaim until my transplant – and with that came some unexpected 'befores' and 'afters' of my own. There are 'before' books, music, photos, people and places. I hear a song and think, 'Oh, that's a before song' or 'That's a before book'; before my transplant, before a friend died, before cancer. I've been admonished for living in the past, but I learnt long ago that the past lives in me and it has inextricably grafted me to my future.

As I write this, I am forty-six, which means I've been writing this memoir for thirty-five years. Life has torn me apart in the literal sense, and from a very young age, I believe that my body was made to be broken.

Every day since my transplant, I have thought about my donor and her family, and after seventeen years, I decide to see if I can find out who she is. Mum and I have talked for years about going into Births, Deaths and Marriages to see if we can find her, so armed with what information I have, I drive to the State Library. I walk into a sleepy little room, and sort through reels of microfiche until I find the date of my donor's death. My heart is in my mouth and my gut drops through the floor. I gently feed the reel into the machine and the front-page blares, 'Clinton set to expand war against terrorists' with a picture of Bill Clinton on one side and Osama Bin Laden on the other, a map of the Middle East floating between them. This is three years before September 11, and there is a sense of unease as I read the headline, knowing what's coming.

I have always known rudimentary details about my donor, but never her name or age. I always expected all of these details to remain a lifelong mystery. Once I find her name, I do an internet search on the off chance there's any other information about her. I'm shocked to find a photo of her grave. I'm even more shocked to see a photo of her. I knew she had red hair. Don't ask me how I knew, I just did. She was married, but with her maiden name we share the same initials. She was twenty-two and we were born in the same year. It takes me by surprise that she was married. At twenty-two. Her funeral notice reads 'tragically taken' because she was. She was ripped away from her family in the most heavy-hearted of circumstances. But then she gave. She gave me – and others – life.

My ears catch the low hum of people scrolling through microfiche around me, and I begin to cry. Being able to put a name and a face to the woman who saved my life is a level of intense sorrow I had sorely underestimated. I take photos of her death notice and her grave and send them to Mum. I drive home in a daze, and call Mum when I get home. I don't know how to feel, but that night I have the most restful sleep I've had in months.

At the time, I'm blogging, and I share that I've found my donor. The following day, my inbox blows up with transplant recipients asking how I found them, and I warn them that while this is a door that can easily be opened, it's one that can never be closed. I advise them to assess their mental wellbeing before they pursue the unknown. I am in a good place mentally, yet I still feel shell shocked. While I feel that I've found a piece of myself, I wonder if I've been reckless. Sometimes doors stay closed for good reason.

Just before my twenty-year Transplanniversary I resolve to visit the cemetery where my donor is interred. On a Saturday morning in late August, I sit at my kitchen table with a cup of tea and write what feel like empty words into a card. It seems absurd to write 'thank you', but I write it anyway. I pick roses from my garden, Mum picks some crucifix orchids, and we make a little posy that I clutch for the ninety-minute drive. We arrive at the tiny cemetery just as a squall picks up, and after a couple of minutes of walking around, Dad gently calls out, 'She's over here.'

My stomach lurches, and as I walk over to where my parents are standing, I feel a stream of sick rise in my throat. From having seen her gravestone in newspaper tributes over the years, I know the photo well, but it's still a shock to see her face; to actually be there with her. And yet not with her.

Up close, she is effortlessly radiant and seems to be all-knowing as a corona of light floats on top of her head. She exudes grace, and there's a tenderness behind her eyes.

As it happens, we're not the only ones paying our respects this weekend. A large white envelope with her name on it sits sentinel at her grave, weighed down with rocks so it won't be carried away by the wind. After a few minutes, I press down through my thighs to get to ground, place my hands onto the stone and close my eyes.

There is a staggering sense of reverence, and I feel what a place of pain this is. But it's also a place of peace – a place of renewal, rest and love. Over and over again, I whisper, 'Thank you, thank you, thank you.' When I stand up and look across to my parents, Mum is crying, and Dad's face is red. They offer their thanks, and Dad walks over to plant a kiss where my hands have been.

'It's all because of you,' he says.

Not expecting this, I begin to cry. Dad clears his throat, pulls his sunglasses down and walks on.

The following Saturday night, I have a party with my closest family and friends, many of whom were at the hospital the night of my surgery. After we've toasted my donor, my father delivers an impromptu speech, breaking down as he recalls the emotion of our visit to the cemetery. Later, I speak to Bec, Mel and Tammy who were there when I was sitting up on the gurney as I was wheeled into theatre, screaming.

'It was like listening to the end of the world,' one says, the others nodding in agreement.

'I'm so sorry. That would've been awful,' I say.

'Don't be sorry!' they chorus, swaddling me into an embrace.

Is it possible to love someone you do not know? To love someone you will never meet? To love a refugee fleeing war is to love a stranger. Is it not so peculiar to find yourself loving a stranger and their family who saved your life? For me, it is the deepest kind of love. My donor family gave me space for all of the love I had left over from so much loss. If anyone is worthy of love, it is them. And in the end, as I sit writing this with my hound at my feet, maybe I am too.

In 2022, I'm snuggling with my dog, Billie, my nose in a book, when I get a call from Dad. He has the flu, and being a stoic baby boomer male, he never complains and would rather surrender a limb than see a doctor for something so puerile as the flu. But today I can tell he's on the verge of tears. 'How did you do it?'

'Do what?'

'Everything. High school. How did you do high school? I'm in agony. Every time I cough, my whole body hurts. My back. My chest. Jesus Christ, I don't know how you did it.'

I tell him that because I'd been born sick, I had never known any different.

'Well, I just want to say ... well bloody done. I still don't know how you managed.'

'I just did. I was used to it. You know, it was just always there.'

'I know you were sick, but I never really got it. And I'm not even that sick. How did you function with pneumonia?'

'I just did.'

'And you were always so happy. Never bloody complained. Well ... hats off to you, love. Guts effort.'

We exchange 'I love you's as all my family do when we hang up the phone or leave each other.

I burst into tears.

Acknowledgements

When I began writing *Breath* in 2018, pulling on tendrils of memory and committing them to the page felt like a solitary – even brutal – act, and yet I knew I needed to do it.

To my lifeline, anchor and ballast – Mum, Dad and Nikki – your love, support and belief in me is limitless, has held me together and sustained me from the beginning. I love you.

To my mainstays and biggest loves who have seen every version of me and beyond – Bec, Sharon, Tammy, Mel, Laura, Eliza, Elly, Megan, Sir Stephen, Kate, Shelbo, Lachy, Dylan, Toby, Ivan, Leo, Mel O, Alicia, Geyonce, Paul T, Kate and George (my human constellation Orion) – thank you for your love, faith and patience. Most of all – thank you for staying and bringing me back time and time again.

To my maniacs – Tim, Dan, Mitch and Sam – being your auntie is an honour because you make my world a happier place. To know you is to love you.

Thank you to my agent, the inimitable Jeanne Ryckmans who courageously took me on after only having read one essay. Not everyone gets to have their agent as both wise counsel and dear friend.

To my Charlie's Angels (and my devil) – Michele Seminara, Jo Butler, Kris Olsson, Beejay Silcox and Robbie Coburn – for being champions of my writing and indeed, this book.

I am overjoyed that *Breath* found its forever home at UQP. My publisher, Madonna Duffy, has been a gentle, kind and passionate shepherd in bringing this book to life. It's been such an immense privilege working with you.

I have so much gratitude for my editors, Jacqueline Blanchard and Vanessa Pellatt, who honed the book you hold in your hands. Editors are the unsung heroes of publishing and I salute you.

I wouldn't be at this juncture of life without the hundreds of people who have kept me alive: my CF and lung transplant doctors, transplant coordinators, nurses, phlebotomists (you have my heart, or at least, my deep brachial artery), oncologists, plastic surgeons, theatre and oncology nurses, anaesthetists, physiotherapists, respiratory scientists, pharmacists, hospital schoolteachers, spiritual carers (I see you), receptionists, wardies/orderlies and cleaners, meal people, and volunteers from all of the hospitals I've called home at some stage – the Royal Children's Hospital, the Mater, the Prince Charles Hospital and the Royal Brisbane and Women's Hospital.

Thanks to my Pineapple Crew for keeping me caffeinated and endlessly entertained.

Many thanks to *Kill Your Darlings* for publishing the essay, 'Twice Dead' in 2021 and Varuna for a 2022 Writer's Space Fellowship.

If it seems odd to thank my dog, then odd I shall be. To Billie, my human canine dyad who just so happened to be the missing piece of my puzzle – I adore you and owe you many treats for being my memoir and thesis support dog.

This book is for all of my CF friends who are no longer earthside, of which there are multitudes. You live on.

Finally, and perhaps most poignantly, *Breath* is dedicated to my donor and her family – I owe you everything. Thank you, thank you, thank you.